THE
ILLUSTRATED
DICTIONARY
of
BOATING
TERMS

The
ILLUSTRATED
DICTIONARY
of
BOATING
TERMS

2000 ESSENTIAL TERMS
FOR SAILORS
& POWERBOATERS

JOHN ROUSMANIERE

W. W. Norton & Company
New York   London

For information about permission to reproduce selections from this book,
write to Permissions, W. W. Norton & Company, Inc.,
500 Fifth Avenue, New York, NY 10110

The text of this book is composed in Centaur with the display set in Gill Sans.
Composition by FoggDesign. Manufacturing by Haddon Craftsmen.
Book design by Pamela Fogg. Illustrations by Linda Deming.
Cover illustration courtesy of South Street Seaport Museum.

Library of Congress Cataloging-in-Publication Data
Rousmaniere, John.
    The illustrated dictionary of boating terms : 2000 essential terms for
sailors and powerboaters / by John Rousmaniere. — [Rev. ed.]
        p. cm.
Rev. ed. of: A glossary of modern sailing terms. ©1989.

ISBN 0-393-04649-4

    1. Boats and boating—Dictionaries. I. Rousmaniere, John.
Glossary of modern sailing terms. II. Title.
GV775.R68 1998
797.1'24'03—DC21   97-45938
                                                                      CIP

W. W. Norton & Company, Inc., 500 Fifth Avenue, New York, NY 10110
http://www.wwnorton.com

W. W. Norton & Company Ltd., 10 Coptic Street, London WC1A 1PU

1 2 3 4 5 6 7 8 9 0

To Dad, again and always

INTRODUCTION

FROM ABACK TO ZULU, including words as new as bowrider and as old as starboard, here is the current language of pleasure boating—more than 2,000 new, recent, and classic terms and their cousins that today's power-boaters and sailors rely on to make their way safely and happily upon America's inland and coastal waters. In writing these definitions, I have drawn from my own broad experience and reading. To be sure that the book is up-to-date I also carefully reviewed recent issues of several American power and sail magazines and incorporated the new words I found there.

In the interest of full disclosure, I should indicate my two main prejudices. First, I generally do not prefer land-bound words when good seagoing terms do the job. I cringe at the current trend of saying **drive** in place of **steer**—a healthy, clear seafaring term vastly preferred to its clanky automotive cousin. Second, I favor gender-neutral language when it is not awkward. Because boating language was created by males, its traditional vocabulary is peppered with terms like **helmsman** and **man overboard,** but today these words are wrong about half the time. Therefore I suggest more accurate and inclusive terms, but only if they are not ungainly, for instance **steerer** and **crew overboard** (in place of "helmsperson" and "person overboard").

Regardless of my preferences, all options are included. You'll find **helmsman** and **man overboard** here (and even **drive**).

A Few Words
About a Living Language

To people who complain that recommending **steerer** over **helmsman** is taking liberties, I can only reply that there already have been plenty of liberties taken. The bubbling up of new terms is one of the facts (and, I think, glories) of the boating language.

Developed spontaneously wherever boats go, the sailor's and powerboater's language is fascinating and often perplexing in its ingenuity and variety. Of course, many terms have universal meaning because they are crucial to safety and good seamanship. **Starboard** always refers to the right side of the boat, **port** to the left. Any skipper who confuses the two will immediately get into trouble. The same rule applies to **bow** and **stern, sheet** and **halyard, forward** and **aft,** and a number of other words it is best not to confuse or forget in moments of difficulty. But otherwise, there is a broad choice of accepted terms and meanings—many of them extremely inventive and appealing. Some old narrow usages are being expanded. A **hawsepipe** or **hawse,** for example, traditionally is a hole in the bow for the anchor rode or for a **hawser,** which is an especially large docking or towing line. We still have **hawsepipes,** except that today, they also include holes in a small powerboat's rail near the stern for leading docking lines. Same word, different ends of the boat, and pretty much the same meaning.

Some terms are close to poetic. Everybody is familiar with the term "raging storm." In the Bahamas, the storm itself is called a **rage.** And when boats are difficult to steer, just like stubborn people they are called **cranky.** Other words are wonderfully picturesque. Sailors use a variety of expressions to describe sailing extremely close to the wind, with the sails luffing slightly. Some say they are **pinching** or

squeezing—literally compressing the wind between the sails and the axis of its direction. Other sailors speak of **feathering;** as they luff, the sails lift and fall like a feather in the breeze.

And there always is the beauty of simple pragmatism. A very light sail set in a calm in order to pick up gossamer wisps of wind is a **windseeker.** When a powerboat rolls from side to side, she is described as doing a **chine walk**— putting down one chine (the meeting place of the bottom and side), then the other, then the other. When you go out in a boat during the winter, you are **frostbiting.** And there can be no better name for a strong fitting to take a docking line than **samson post,** which, unlike the Biblical strongman, cannot be weakened by a haircut. In many parts of the boating world, powerboats are either **cabin cruisers** or **open boats.** But recently, in an interview on National Public Radio, an official at a lock on a Texas river used the term **deck boat** when referring to a larger powerboat. **Deck boats,** he said, have "fishing towers and American flags and everything."

The origins of some terms are fascinating. Take **starboard.** In ancient times, before the invention of the rudder, German and Norse boats were steered by oars that were located on the right-hand *bord,* or side, presumably because most people are right-handed. In order to avoid breaking this valuable oar, when they docked seamen put the boat's left-hand side against the port's wharf. In time, the boat's right side came to be called the steering side, or *"steorbord"* (the ancestor of our **starboard**) and the left side became the port side. Other terms honor the inventors or the place of origin of equipment. The **Cunningham,** for example, was reportedly invented by a fellow named Briggs Cunningham, and the **genoa jib** was first used publicly during a race in the Mediterranean off Genoa, Italy.

Then there are words whose sheer variety or complexity can make them confusing. Some meanings share a single word (see **run**), and a few terms have odd pronunciations (a **pendant** is a "pennant," a **mainsail** a "main-*sul*"). The following terms all mean "to alter course toward the wind direction": **head up, harden up, come up, round up, freshen your wind, sharpen up, sharpen your wind, heat it up.** On every boat you will hear one or two of them, each within a specific context.

Even the act of naming a boat is replete with choices. As you will see in the section **boat names,** your dream vessel may be "**the** *Pageant*" and an "it" if you think of it as a great ship, or "*Pageant*" and "she" if the relationship is more intimate.

These shifts, like so many in the nautical language, are subtle, in common use, and generally acceptable. Read on, and decide for yourself.

JOHN ROUSMANIERE
STAMFORD, CONNECTICUT
NOVEMBER 1997

THIS IS A THOROUGHLY revised and updated edition of *A Glossary of Modern Sailing Terms*, first published by Dodd, Mead & Co. in 1976 with 1,200 terms and later revised with 1,500 terms. This new edition is a completely new book. Not only does it incorporate dozens of power-boating terms, but almost all the definitions from the earlier editions have been rewritten.

To make sure the text is current and relevant, I carefully consulted several 1997 issues of the following magazines: *Blue Water Sailing, Boating, Boating World, Cruising World, MotorBoating & Sailing, Practical Sailor, Sail, Sailing World,* and *Yachting.*

The original edition was inspired by the late Bob Rimington, the former editor and publisher of *Yachting* magazine, and Bill Robinson, then *Yachting*'s editor. I thank the following for their assistance: Harvey Loomis, Leah Ruth Robinson Rousmaniere, Carleton Mitchell, and Admiral Robert J. McNitt, each of whom made helpful comments about one or more terms; John Barstow, my editor at W.W. Norton, who proposed this revision; Jenny Dunham, my agent at Russell & Volkening; and Rick Bonaparte, who provided valuable production assistance.

Errors or omissions are my own responsibility. Suggestions for future editions may be sent to me care of c/o Boating Books Department, W.W. Norton & Co., 500 Fifth Ave., New York, NY 10110.

A GUIDE TO USING THIS DICTIONARY

- *If you see an undefined term in one definition, it's usually defined in its own definition.* For example:

  measurement system A rating rule.

  If you don't know what a rating rule is, look for it under "R".

- *These words are specific to boats.* A small number of basic meteorological and mechanical terms appear, but only in a boating context.

- *A single definition covers alternative terms.* For example:

  sound signal, whistle signal, horn signal The sound made by a whistle or horn.

  And under **whistle signal** and **horn signal** you will find:

  horn signal See sound signal.

  whistle signal See sound signal.

- *If you can't find a two-word term under one word, try the other.* You'll find **anchor rode** under **anchor** and **sidestay** under **stay**.

- *Large families of related terms are grouped.* See, for instance, **anchor, fore (forward),** and **propeller.**

- *Many words serve both as nouns and as verbs.*

- *Some words have multiple meanings.* These are sorted out in the definition. The simple word **run** has five meanings.

- *Optional expressions are included but preferences are suggested.* The first term is the preferred term.

aback With the sails trimmed on the windward side, or backed. A boat is **caught aback** when the wind suddenly shifts and the sails are trimmed to the windward side.

abaft Behind, toward the stern. **Abaft the beam** is the area between abeam and astern. Compare with aft.

abandon ship To leave a sinking, burning, or otherwise fatally distressed vessel. An **abandon ship bag** (ditch bag, grab bag) is a container of emergency and survival gear prepared by the crew to take with them if they must abandon ship.

abeam, on the beam Directly alongside at right angles to the boat.

able, ability An able boat (able vessel) is especially seaworthy. A **boat's ability** in a particular situation is an evaluation of her speed, comfort, and seaworthiness. **Rough-water ability,** for example, is how she handles waves. Related expressions include **heavy-weather ability, windward (upwind) ability, light-air ability.**

aboard, on board In or on a boat. An object that is **close aboard** is very nearby. To **go aboard** a boat is to go on or in her.

accommodations, accommodation The living area and furniture in a boat, including bunks, heads, and a galley. The

accommodations (accommodation) plan is the yacht designer's scale drawing showing the arrangement of the cabins and furniture.

acockbill(ed), cockbilled Set at an angle. Describes the anchor as it lies on the rail or is hung over the bow, ready to be dropped.

adrift Describes a boat drifting out of control, and loose, unsecured equipment.

advisory See weather alert.

aerodynamics The study of air flow around objects. Compare with hydrodynamics.

afloat Floating.

aft, after At or toward the stern, or behind. An **aft (after) cabin** is a cabin at or near the stern, the **afterbody** the hull near the stern, the **afterdeck** the deck near the stern, the **spinnaker afterguy** a control on a spinnaker pole that leads aft (in contrast to the foreguy, which leads to the foredeck near the bow). Compare with abaft, ahead, fore.

afterguard The boat's captain, navigator, and other officers. In sailing ships the officers historically worked aft near the steering wheel and slept in after cabins, which are more comfortable than cabins near the bow.

aground Stuck on the water's bottom. To **run aground** is to become stuck.

ahead In front of or forward of the bow. A boat **clear ahead** is completely ahead.

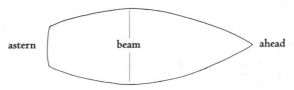

astern beam ahead

ahull Pronounced "ah-*hull*." Stopped and without sails set or power on. To **lie ahull** is to drift without sails or power. Sometimes used as a storm tactic.

aid to navigation, navigation aid A buoy, daybeacon, lighthouse, range, or other charted object in or near the water that identifies channels and helps a crew navigate safely.

air Wind, breeze.

air tank An airtight, watertight compartment that provides buoyancy to keep the boat afloat in case she takes on water.

alee Away from the wind, to leeward. "Hard alee," see hard.

all hands The entire crew.

aloft Above the deck, in the rig.

alongshore, longshore Near shore, coastal.

alongside Next to.

alter course To change the direction in which the boat is steered.

American Boat and Yacht Council, ABYC An organization that recommends standards and practices in boat and boat gear construction.

American Power Boat Association, APBA A governing body of powerboat racing in the United States.

American Bureau of Shipping, ABS An organization that supervises scantlings for marine construction.

American Outboard Federation, AOF A governing body for racing by boats powered by outboard engines.

America's Cup, the Auld Mug, the Cup A trophy for sailboat racing donated by the New York Yacht Club in 1857 "upon the condition that it shall be preserved as a perpetual challenge cup for friendly competition between foreign countries." The oldest international sporting trophy in continuous competition, it is sailed approximately every four years in response to foreign challenges to the last winner. It has been

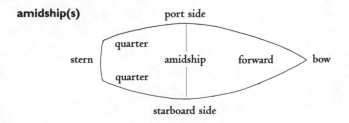

amidship(s)

port side

quarter

stern   amidship   forward   bow

quarter

starboard side

held by yacht clubs in the United States, Australia, and New Zealand.

amidship(s), midship(s) Toward the center of the boat. **Midships section,** see lines.

AMVER See Automated Mutual Assistance Vessel Rescue System.

ANCHOR, HOOK

A metal device that is lowered from the boat on rope or chain (**anchor rode**) and that digs into or lies on the water's bottom and so holds the boat. To **set the anchor** is to help it dig in by pulling hard on the rode. When the **anchor drags,** it springs loose from the bottom, leaving the boat adrift.

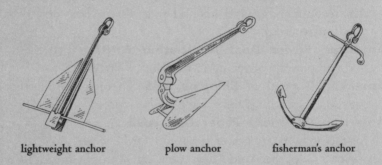

lightweight anchor   plow anchor   fisherman's anchor

All anchors have flukes (points that dig into the bottom or grab rocks) and a shank (a vertical bar). Many also have a stock (a horizontal bar that prevents rolling over) and a crown (where the stock, flukes, and/or shank meet). Anchor types include those listed below.

- **Burying-type anchors** hold by digging their flukes into the bottom. Among them are the **lightweight (fluke) anchor** (including the Fortress and Danforth, both of which have stocks) and the heavier stockless **plow anchor (CQR),** Bruce **anchor,** and **mushroom anchor.**

- Another type is the **kedge (stock, nonburying) anchor.** The best example is the large, heavy, cross-shaped **fisherman's anchor (yachtsman's anchor)**, which holds the boat with its weight and by snagging rocks.

- A third type is the **lunch hook anchor,** a small, light anchor used temporarily; one kind is the **grapnel anchor (grapnel hook).**

- A **storm anchor** is an unusually heavy anchor of either the burying or kedge family, reserved for use in strong winds.

- The **helix anchor** is a steel shaft screwed into the bottom for use usually with moorings.

- A **sea anchor** does not hook the boat to the bottom but rather provides drag against drift. See sea anchor.

The anchor and rode have associated equipment:

- The **anchor light** (riding light) is illuminated when the boat is anchored at night outside a special anchorage; see anchorage. The anchor rode sometimes leads over an **anchor (stem) roller.** An **anchor sentinel** (weighted dolly, kellet) is a weight slid partway down the anchor rode in order to increase the anchor's catenary, or sag, which improves the anchor's holding power. The **anchor well** is a locker recessed in the deck for stowing the anchor.

An **anchor alarm** is a feature of a GPS or other electronic navigation device or a depthsounder that sounds an audible alarm when the anchor drags and the boat shifts position. To **buoy the anchor** is to attach a buoy to it so it and its rode can be found if they must be abandoned. The **anchor watch** is the crew awake and on deck as lookouts while the boat is anchored. See "straight up and down" and swinging room.

anchorage A place for anchoring. A **good (safe) anchorage** is protected by land and has relatively shallow water and good holding ground, without weed or rocks. A **poor (unsafe) anchorage** is otherwise. A **special anchorage** is an area set aside by the government for anchoring and mooring boats.

anemometer A device that measures the wind's speed and displays it on an indicator.

angle of attack The angle between a sail and the wind or between the keel or rudder and the boat's course.

antifouling paint Paint applied to a boat's underbody to prevent growth of barnacles and weed.

apparent wind The strength and direction of the wind as felt in a moving boat. It is the true wind modified by the boat's movement. An **apparent wind indicator (AWI)** shows the direction of the apparent wind. Compare with true wind.

appendage A fin—the centerboard, keel, rudder, or skeg—under the boat that helps with steering and provides lateral resistance (and provides ballast, in the case of the keel). Most keels and skegs are fixed in place, while centerboards are retractable and rudders turn. Appendages usually have foil shapes to improve the flow of water around them and to provide lift.

arch, radar arch A frame over a cockpit, bridge, or deck on which antennas, radars and radar reflectors, solar panels, lights, awnings, horns, and other items are mounted out of the way of the crew.

around the buoys Racing for only a few hours on race courses with short legs defined by turning marks. Compare with ocean race.

ashore To or on the shore, or land.

aspect ratio The numerical ratio between a sail's, keel's, or other object's height and its width. A relatively narrow sail has a **high aspect ratio**, a wide one a **low aspect ratio**.

astern Behind or abaft the stern. A boat **clear astern** is completely astern.

asymmetrical Having sides with different shapes or lengths.

An **asymmetrical spinnaker** is longer on one leech than on the other. An **asymmetrical leeboard** in a scow or an **asymmetrical hull** in a catamaran (for example a Hobie Cat) is more rounded on one side than the other.

asymmetrical spinnaker

athwartships, thwartships, 'thwartships Across the boat, either inboard (toward the centerline) or outboard (toward the rail).

attached flow Air or water flowing smoothly over a sail or appendage. Compare with stall.

Auld Mug See America's Cup.

Automated Mutual Assistance Vessel Rescue System, AMVER A search-and-rescue (SAR) system run by the U.S. Coast Guard.

automatic pilot, autopilot See self-steerer.

Automatic Ship Identification transponder, ASI transponder An option in a VHF radio that alerts the crew to nearby vessels.

auxiliary 1) An engine that provides motive power in a sailboat, or electrical power in any boat. 2) An **auxiliary sailboat (auxiliary)** is a sailboat with an engine.

awash When waves wash over an object.

aweigh See weigh anchor.

Awlgrip A widely used brand of polyurethane paint that serves as a glossy, tough coating for topsides.

awning A cover providing shade.

B

babystay See stay.

back, aback 1) On the wrong side or in the contrary direction. When a sail is **backed** or **aback** it is trimmed to windward rather than to leeward, as is usual. A **back eddy** is a current flowing against the main current. 2) A counterclockwise wind shift. When the wind shifts from north to west it **backs** or is a **backing wind**. Compare with veer. 3) **Back off**, see pawl.

back down To go backward or stern first.

backstay See stay.

backwind 1) Air flowing aft off one sail and into another. The second sail is **backwinded**. 2) A type of dirty air.

baggywrinkle A bushy winding of yarns secured to a spreader or stay to help prevent chafe on sails.

bail To remove bilge water with a bucket or sponge. **Bailers (self-bailers)** are retractable sluices in the bilge of a boat through which bilge water drains when the boat is moving rapidly.

balance To adjust the weights, rigging, or sails so a boat handles easily. A **balanced (well-balanced) boat** is one that is easily steered without excess weather or lee helm.

bale A curved metal strap, usually on a spar for hanging a block.

ballast Weight in a sailboat that resists heeling force and thereby improves stability. **Fixed ballast,** usually consisting of lead, may be **internal ballast** in the bilge or **external ballast** in the keel. **Movable ballast** is weight that can be moved on deck to the windward side, for example the crew or **water ballast,** which is water pumped into a tank at the windward rail.

ball valve See seacock.

bank A large area of shallow water.

bar An area of shoal water at the entrance to a river or harbor.

Barber hauler A line used to adjust the athwartships lead of a jibsheet. Invented by Merrit Barber.

bareboat See charter.

barge 1) A large flat-bottomed vessel for carrying cargo, towed behind or pushed by a tugboat. 2) To force an opening between boats. 3) A derogatory term for a boat that means ugly and slow.

barney post A post in a sailboat's cockpit, to which the mainsheet and other sail controls are led.

barometer, aneroid barometer, barograph, the glass An instrument that displays atmospheric pressure in inches or millibars and therefore is useful in predicting weather. A **barograph (recording barometer)** records barometric readings over several days.

bass boat A low flat-bottomed powerboat without a cabin, smaller than about 20 feet, powered by a large outboard motor as well as by a small trolling engine. It may have a fishing chair.

batten A thin wooden or synthetic slat inserted into a pocket in the leech of a sail to help the sail hold its shape. A **full-length batten** extends the width of the sail.

batten down To prepare a boat for

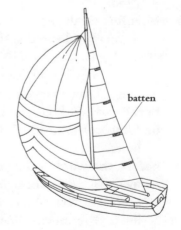

batten

rough weather by closing all ports, hatches, and other openings.

B.C. See beach club and boat club.

beach boat A boat small and light enough to be easily pulled up on shore.

beach club, B.C. A boating and swimming club.

beacon See daybeacon.

beam 1) A boat's width, often abbreviated **bm.** The **maximum beam** is the greatest width. A **beamy** boat is relatively wide for her length. Something that is **abeam** or **on the beam** is at a right angle to the boat. A **beam wind** or **beam sea** comes directly from the side. When a boat is on a **beam reach,** the wind is a **beam wind** or **on the beam.** When a boat is **on her beam's end** she is heeled dangerously far. 2) A structural support for the deck, often **deck beam.**

bear away, bear off Head off.

bearing A direction between objects, for example between your boat and a lighthouse. A **compass bearing** is in magnetic degrees as shown on a compass. A **relative bearing** is the inscribed angle between the objects. A crewmember **takes a bearing** or **cuts a bearing.** The **range and bearing** to a way-point or other point is the distance and course to it.

beat Sail close-hauled. A **dead beat** is a leg directly into the wind.

Beaufort Scale Pronounced "bofort scale." A system for estimating wind speed and describing sea conditions, developed in the late eighteenth century by Sir Francis Beaufort, a British admiral. The system has 12 categories, called "Forces," ranging from Force 1 (calm) to Force 12 (hurricane).

becalmed Without wind.

bedding compound A thick paste used to seal joints and fill holes.

before the wind Sailing on a run, with the wind astern.

belay 1) To cleat. A **belaying pin,** found in many traditional sail-boats, is a vertical metal rod used in place of a cleat to secure lines. 2) Terminate. **"Belay that"** is an order to stop an activity or to stop talking.

bell 1) **Bell buoy,** see buoy, buoyage. 2) **Ship's bells,** see ship's clock.

below, belowdeck(s) In the cabin or under the deck.

bend 1) To **bend on** a line or sail is to attach it so it is ready for use. To **unbend** it is to detach it. 2) A knot used to tie lines to each other. 3) A **bendy mast** is easily bent or curved in order to change the shape of the mainsail. **Prebend** is bend put into the mast by adjusting the rigging before sails are hoisted.

Bergstrom and Ridder rig, B&R rig A mast with backswept spreaders that provide support fore and aft as well as athwartships. Often seen on very large cruising sailboats.

Bermuda Race A family of sailboat races from the U.S. East Coast to Bermuda (a distance of approximately 700 miles), the oldest of which is the one from Newport, R.I., sponsored in even-numbered years by the Cruising Club of America.

Bermudian rig See rig.

berth 1) For a person, a bed in a boat. Also bunk. A **settee berth** is a bench that is convertible into a berth. A **pilot berth** is a narrow berth under the side deck. A **quarter berth** is under the afterdeck. A **pipe berth** has a pipe frame and can be folded up against the hull. 2) For a boat, the place where she is moored or docked. 3) A **wide berth** is a margin of safety. 4) A **crew's berth** is a position in a crew.

bight 1) See line. 2) A **bight of land** is a bend in the shore or coastline.

bilge The lowest part of the hull. **Bilge water** collects there due to leaks or spray. Water is removed by a hand-operated **manual bilge pump** or by an **electric bilge pump** activated by hand or by a float switch, an electric switch triggered by the rise of a small buoy in the bilge. The float switch may also set off an audible **bilge alarm.** A **bilge sniffer** senses the presence of gas fumes in the bilge and sounds an alarm. A **bilge blower** exhausts gas fumes. **Bilge keel,** see keel.

Bimini top, Bimini A removable awning that swings up over the cockpit.

Bimini top

bin Stowage compartment.

binnacle Pronounced "binakel." A support for a compass, usually the main compass in the cockpit near the helm. A **binnacle compass** is a compass in a binnacle.

bitt, samson post A post for securing docking and mooring lines. Compare with bollards.

bitter end See line.

black flag A signal flown by a race committee in a sailboat race to indicate that a boat is disqualified for starting the race prematurely.

blade 1) A **propeller blade.** 2) A rudder or centerboard. 3) A tall, narrow jib that fills the foretriangle and does not overlap the mast or shrouds.

blanket To obstruct a sailboat's wind and slow her down. See cover and slam dunk.

blazer, blue blazer A blue jacket. It is the closest thing there is to a pleasure boater's uniform.

blind man's test A way to examine a wire for frayed strands by rubbing it with a hand or rag.

blister See fiberglass.

BLOCK

A pulley on a boat for supporting or directing line or wire. A roller (sheave, pronounced "shiv") is hung between two supports (cheeks) either on a pin (sheave pin) or on ball bearings. To **reeve a line through a block** is to lead it between the cheeks.

There are many types of blocks:

- A **snatch block** can be opened at its side to receive line. A

snatch block   double block   triple block   fixed block

fixed block cannot be opened.

- A **single block** has one sheave, a **double block** two sheaves, and so on. A **becket block** has a fixed eye as well as one or more sheaves. A **bullet block** is very small. A **cheek block** is always open on one side. A **turning block** redirects a line. A **foot block** is a turning block lying on its side on the deck. A **ratchet block** has a mechanism that permits the sheave to turn in only one direction and so snubs (takes much of the load off) the line.

- **Block and tackle,** handy billy—see tackle.

blower Bilge blower.
blowover A capsize by a powerboat at high speed when air catches under the hull.
blue water Far offshore or off soundings, where the water tends to be darker than near shore. A **bluewater boat** or **bluewater sailor** is suitable for ocean sailing far from land.
bluff-bowed See full-ended.
bm Beam.
board 1) To go on a boat is to **go aboard.** 2) A tack when sailing close-hauled; the **starboard board** is the starboard tack. 3) Centerboard. 4) A **sailboard.**
board boat A low, lightweight sailing dinghy.
boarding gate, boarding ladder A gate or ladder that facilitates going aboard a boat.

boardsailing, windsurfing Sailing a sailboard. The sailor is a **boardsailor** or **windsurfer**.

boat A smaller vessel. The difference between a boat and a ship is that a boat is small enough to be placed aboard a ship, but a ship is too large to be placed aboard a boat. "To boat" is not a verb. Use **"I'm going boating,"** not "I boat."

boat club, B.C. A kind of yacht club, often less formal.

boater 1) A person who regularly goes boating for pleasure. A boater who usually sails is a sailor; a **powerboater** is one who uses powerboats. 2) A traditional straw hat.

boat handling The skills of steering and maneuvering a boat.

boathook A pole with a hook on its end for grabbing objects, such as a line in the water.

BOAT NAMES

Boats are unique—part living being and part object. Because the balance is unclear, the naming of boats is disputed territory.

- **"She" versus "it."** The tradition that a boat is (or represents) a woman who brings luck to the crew goes back to the ancient Egyptians, and so the female pronouns "she" and "her" have long been used to refer to a boat. Today an increasing number of people prefer "it," which, while short on personality, does not risk controversy by generalizing about gender. This usage is not unprecedented. There is a long tradition of using "it" in reference to a commercial ship or naval vessel, as well as to a vessel's design. Both "she" and "it" are acceptable. The author refers to a pleasure boat as "she."

- **"The."** Many people who enjoy being part of the naval and seafaring tradition often use the article "the" before the name of a pleasure boat, just as professional mariners do with the names of ships (for example "my boat is **the** *Elixir*"). However, those who believe that pleasure boats are distinct from commercial craft do not use "the" ("my boat is *Elixir*").

Both usages are accepted and widely used. The author usually does not use the prefix "the" before a boat's name.

- In print, **boat names** usually are underlined, italicized, or printed in all capital letters (Elixir, *Elixir*, or ELIXIR). A **class of boat** is known by a brand name and length, for example Sabre 40 or 40-foot Sabre, without italics or another typographical note.

boat show An exhibit of boats and boating equipment for sale.

boat speed A boat's speed through the water in knots or miles per hour, as indicated on the speedometer. It differs from the **speed (velocity) made good (SMG, VMG),** which is the speed relative to geography, takes all factors into account, and is displayed on the GPS or Loran-C. Compare with made good.

boatswain, bosun Pronounced *"bo*-sun." The crewmember assigned to maintenance. **Boatswain's gear** consists of a knife, small tools, needles, thread, tape, and other items for repairs. A **boatswain's chair (boatswain's strap)** is a seat, strap, or sling on which a crewmember is hauled aloft by a halyard or gantline to inspect or repair rigging or to do other chores. A **boatswain's hook** is a pole with a dull-pointed hook at the end for retrieving mooring buoys and other objects in the water. Compare with gaff.

boat tape Waterproof or water-resistant tape.

boatyard, shipyard, yard A commercial operation where boats are built, painted, stored, or repaired.

bobstay A stay or chain running from the end of a bowsprit to the stem to help support the sprit. It may run over a strut extending downward from the bowsprit (dolphin striker).

body The hull. The **body (canoe body, underbody)** is the area of the hull that lies below the water.

body of water A sea, lake, harbor, river, or other area of water.

bollards Two adjacent vertical posts (heads) for tying docking lines. Compare with bitt, samson post.

boltrope Rope sewn to the edge of a sail to give it shape and strength and to allow it to be fed into a grooved headstay or mast. The boltrope is the only true "rope" afloat, because all other lengths of cordage in use on a boat are referred to as "lines."

bomb A meteorological term describing a storm in which the barometer reading drops extremely rapidly, at a rate of 1 millibar (0.03 inch) an hour or more for a 24-hour period.

boom The spar that holds out a sail at its foot, or bottom edge. When the sail is not hoisted, the boom may be held up by a **boom crutch (boom crotch),** a temporarily rigged support; compare with gallows frame.

boomkin A short strut extending aft from the transom to support the permanent backstay or other gear and keep it clear of the boom.

boom vang, vang, kicking strap, kicker, boom jack A block and tackle or rod that holds the boom down against the lifting force of the sail. A **supporting vang** holds the boom down and also up when the sail is not set.

boottop A painted stripe on the topside, just above the waterline.

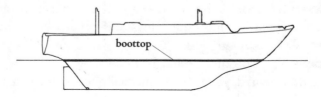

bosun See boatswain.

bottom 1) The **water's bottom** is the land under water. Where it is exposed at low tide is the hard. 2) The **boat's bottom** is her underbody or the underside of her hull.

bow Rhymes with "cow." The very front of the boat. **On the bow** is just to the side of the bow. A **bow line** is a docking line led to shore from the bow. A **bow wave** is the wave kicked up by the bow. A **bow rail** is a railing around the foredeck of a powerboat. A **bowsprit** is a permanent pole or platform extending forward of the bow for securing the anchor or jib tack. The **bow light** shines over the bow. A **bow roller** (stem roller) is a large sheave over which the anchor rode is led. To moor (anchor) **bow-to** is to have the bow nearest the wharf (anchor). A **bow thruster** is a device for steering the bow of a large vessel when maneuvering near piers and in close quarters. Compare with prow.

Bowditch Nathaniel Bowditch's book *American Practical Navigator.*

bowman The crewmember in a sailboat who does the work of handling sails, anchors, and other gear at the bow.

bowrider A runabout with a seating area in the bow.

bowsprit See bow.

braid See rope.

brass, brasswork A soft brown metal traditionally used throughout boats, but generally any metal surface that must be regularly cleaned and polished. Compare with brightwork.

breakdown Rigging or hull damage.

breaker, breaking wave See wave.

break out To take a piece of gear out of stowage and put it into use.

breakwater, jetty, mole A man-made wall in the water that provides protection for a harbor.

breast line A docking line leading directly abeam.

breeze Wind.

bridge, fly bridge, flying bridge A steering platform located a level above a powerboat's deck.

bridge deck The deck between the cockpit and the cabin in a monohull sailboat and between hulls in a multihull.

bridle An arrangement of several lines or wires

fly bridge

used for hoisting or rigging.

brightwork Brass gear and varnished surfaces that must be kept polished.

Bristol fashion, shipshape and Bristol fashion In best possible condition.

broach To head up (**broach to windward**) or off (**broach to leeward**) sharply and out of control.

broad off the bow About 45 degrees abaft the bow.

broad on the quarter About 45 degrees abaft the beam.

brummel hook A slotted aluminum or bronze eye used in pairs to secure a line to another object.  One hook links into another when slots are matched.

bulkhead 1) An athwartships-running wall in a boat. A **structural bulkhead** strengthens the hull and deck, and their attachments. A **watertight bulkhead (collision bulkhead)** is a strong wall and door that can be sealed to keep water from pouring into the cabin. Often it is near the bow. 2) On shore, a **bulkhead** (seawall) props up a wharf.

bulwark A low wall on deck to keep out water.

bunk A bed in a boat; also berth. **Bunkboard,** see leecloth.

BUOY, BUOYAGE

An anchored, floating object used in a mooring, as a turning mark in a race course, as an aid to navigation to mark or indicate a channel, and for other purposes. A buoy's identity and visibility are enhanced by its color, shape, and reflector (including a racon). Among aids to navigation are

- A **nun buoy**—red, even-numbered, and conical at the top.

- A **can buoy**—green, odd-numbered, and flat at the top.

- A **lighted buoy**—displays a flashing or fixed white, red, or green light.

- A **sound buoy**—has a whistle, a single-toned bell (**bell buoy**), or a multitoned gong (**gong buoy**).

Other buoys used as aids to navigation indicate dangers, the centers and intersections of channels, anchorages, danger areas, etc. In addition, the **horseshoe buoy** is a personal flotation device (PFD).

Buoyage (buoyage system) is the arrangement of buoys that are aids to navigation to indicate safe water. There are two systems:

1. In the **lateral buoyage system** or **federal system** (used in America), nuns, cans, and other buoys mark the sides or entrances of channels.

2. In the **cardinal buoyage system** (used in Europe), buoys indicate hazards to navigation.

See racon and reflector.

buoyancy In general, the force that keeps an object afloat, but also often refers to the foam, air tanks, or other floatation devices that provide buoyancy. **Personal buoyancy** is a personal flotation device (PFD) or life jacket.

burdened vessel See give way.

burgee A small flag that carries a yacht club's distinctive symbol.

butt, heel The very bottom of a mast. See step.

by the lee

by the lee Sailing on a run with the wind coming over the same side as the boom, from slightly on the leeward side.

cabin An enclosed area in a boat that can be shut off from the elements. A **cabin cruiser** (sedan cruiser) is a power cruiser with a comfortable cabin large enough to live, eat, and sleep in. A **cuddy cabin** (cuddy) is the smallest cabin, with barely enough space for people to sit.

cable 1) A heavy rope or chain. 2) Two hundred yards, or ¹⁄₁₀ nautical mile.

call To watch and report on a development, for example the trim of a sail or the location of a nearby boat.

calm No wind and no waves. A **dead calm** or **flat calm** is the most extreme calm.

camber A sail's draft or relative fullness.

can, can buoy See buoy, buoyage.

Canadian Boating Federation The organization governing powerboat racing in Canada.

Canadian Yachting Association, CYA The organization governing sailboat racing in Canada.

canister See life raft.

canoe body, underbody The area of the hull that lies below the water.

cant, canting To swing from side to side. A **canting keel** or

canting rudder swings so it is vertical as the boat heels.

canvas Sails. **Cruising canvas** consists of relatively small sails generally used when cruising. **Racing canvas** consists of a boat's racing sails, which are larger than cruising sails.

capacity plate A label showing a boat's maximum allowable load in pounds. It is required by law to be installed in small boats.

capsize When any object turns over. When a sailboat capsizes all the way, turning upside down, she turns turtle. The **capsize screening test** is a mathematical formula that estimates a boat's likelihood of capsizing and remaining upside down.

captain The person legally in charge of a vessel.

car An adjustable slide, fairlead, or block that runs on a track or traveler.

cardinal points See compass.

cardinal buoyage system See buoyage.

careen To intentionally heel a vessel far to one side in order to get her off a shallow spot or to work on her bottom.

carline Structural supports for the deck around a hatch or other opening.

carry away To break.

catamaran

carry way, carry her (the boat's) way To keep moving on momentum after the sails are doused or luffed or the engine is taken out of gear.

car top To transport a boat on an automobile's roof.

cast off To free a line, often in the text of changing tacks, leaving a dock or mooring, or some other maneuver. Compare with ease, let fly, loose, lose, let go, let out, pay out.

catamaran, cat A boat with two

distinct hulls. Compare with cathedral hull, trimaran, tunnel hull.

catboat A traditional, beamy centerboard sailboat with a cat rig.

catboat

catenary A sag in a rope or line. See anchor.

cathedral hull A hull type in which two low tunnels extend from the wide bow aft several feet, but not as far as the stern. These tunnels form three hulls, the outside of which are called sponsons. At the bow the tunnels and sponsons form arches. The sponsons are not as distinct as the hulls in a true catamaran or trimaran, and they do not extend all the way aft, as they do in a tunnel-hulled boat. Compare with catamaran, trimaran, tunnel hull.

cat rig, una rig, unirig A sailboat rig with only a mainsail. See rig.

cat's paw A light puff of wind making a paw-shaped pattern on the water.

caught aback See aback.

caulk To fill seams.

cavitation A partial vacuum at a propeller caused by disturbed water. It makes the propeller less effective. An **anticavitation plate** on an outboard motor protects the propeller from cavitation.

celestial navigation See navigate.

center The locus of forces. The **center of buoyancy** is the locus of a boat's buoyant upward forces, the **center of gravity** of her weighty downward forces. The **center of lateral resistance** is the balance point on her underbody, the **center of effort** of her sail plan.

centerboard, board A fin that drops and retracts through the boat's bottom. It provides resistance against side forces. Because the centerboard can be raised, the boat may venture into shallow water. Most centerboards pivot on **centerboard pins.** Others **(daggerboards)** retract vertically. Centerboards have only enough ballast to hold them down. Centerboards are inside **centerboard trunks.** A **centerboarder** is a boat with a centerboard. A **keel-centerboarder** has a keel and a centerboard. Compare with keel, leeboard.

center-console boat An open powerboat whose steering station is at a console in the cockpit, leaving plenty of space for the crew to move around. Compare with walkaround.

centerline The imaginary straight line that runs fore and aft along the exact center of a boat.

certificate, license A license for operating a commercial vessel. One is the **"six-pack" certificate** for operating boats with six or fewer paying passengers, officially the Operator of Uninspected Passenger Vessel license. Compare with operator's license.

chafe Wear due to rubbing. **Chafe tape** is sturdy tape used to protect against chafe.

chain Metal links often found in the anchor rode. The **chain locker** is a storage area for the anchor rode. A **chain hook** is a metal claw that grabs and secures a chain anchor rode.

chainplates Sturdy metal straps connecting stays to the hull.

change down To set a smaller sail.

channel 1) A radio frequency. 2) An area of navigable water, often marked by aids to navigation. A **channel marker** is a buoy or other aid to navigation indicating the safe channel. A **shipping channel** (shipping lane) is an especially deep channel specified for commercial vessels. It may have a traffic separation scheme.

chantey, sea chantey Pronounced "shanty." A song sung by professional seamen to pace their work. The **chanteyman** traditionally led the songs.

Chapman's, Chapman Piloting *Piloting, Seamanship, and Small*

Boat Handling, an instructional boating book first written in 1922 by Charles F. Chapman.

character boat See traditional boat.

characteristics See light.

Charley Noble, Charlie Noble The chimney of a galley stove with a hood to keep out water. According to tradition, it is named for a certain Captain Charles Noble, who had an unusual passion for keeping his ship's chimneys polished.

chart A nautical map. Also, to note positions and other navigational information on a chart. A **charting system** is a computerized storage and display instrument for charts. The **chart scale** is the actual distance represented by a distance on the chart. **Large-scale charts** (for example, with a scale of 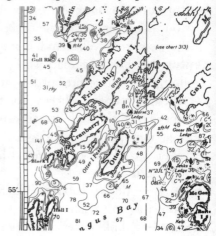 1 inch: 50,000 inches) cover small areas in great detail, while **small-scale charts** (1: 1,000,000 or greater) cover large areas in limited detail. The **chart projection** is the way the globe is represented on flat paper so objects are correctly displayed relative to each other. Since there always will be some distortion, different projections (including Mercator and gnomic) are used, depending on the geographical area and the chart's scale. The **chart table** is a table on which the navigator works on charts. A **Chart Kit** is a trademarked booklet of charts for a region.

charter To rent a boat, or a boat that is rented. On a **bareboat charter** there is no paid crew, while on a **crewed charter** there is one.

cheater A spinnaker staysail.

cheeks See block.

chicken chute See spinnaker.

chine The meeting point of a boat's bottom and side. A **hard chine** has a sharp angle. A **spray chine** near a powerboat's bow deflects spray. A **double chine** is a complex combination of different-shaped chines. When a powerboat does a **chine walk,** she rolls from side to side.

chock A guide for the anchor rode, docking lines, and other lines. A **closed chock** has a latch to keep the line from jumping out, an **open chock** may have small prongs (ears) that retain the line but allow it to be lifted out.

chock-a-block Tightly packed.

chop Low, blunt waves. A **short chop** (short seas) is steep. A **cross chop** (seaway, slop) has waves from different directions, producing a confused pattern.

chord An imaginary line drawn across a sail from luff to leech. The distance from the line to the sail **(chord depth)** indicates the sail's fullness (draft, camber).

chowder A thick fish soup.

chronometer An extremely accurate timepiece.

chute Slang for spinnaker. Derived from "parachute."

Cigarette boat, Cigarette Brand name of an especially low, narrow, fast express cruiser powerboat. Sometimes used as a generic term for such boats.

circle of position, COP See distance off and position.

circumnavigate To go around something. A **circumnavigation** usually is a voyage around the world.

clap on sail Set more sail.

class A group of racing boats governed by the same rules. In **one-design classes** all dimensions are the same. In **restricted classes** many dimensions vary within set limits. In **open classes** most or all dimensions are unrestricted.

classic A term for objects that are old, of high quality, and much admired. Boats or designs that are called **classic yachts** usually are wooden boats with traditional lines, built before about 1960. Among them are boats built by the Herreshoff, Trumpy, Nevins, and Chris-Craft boatyards, and many boats designed by Alden, Sparkman & Stephens, and Rhodes. See traditional boat.

claw off To sail upwind away from a lee shore.

clear Free of restrictions. **Clear air** is wind not affected by other boats or obstructions. When one boat is **clear ahead (clear astern)** of another, they are not overlapped.

cleat To secure a line on one of several types of **cleat.** The line is wrapped several times around a **horn cleat,** wrapped once around a **jam cleat,** laid between the movable sharp jaws of a **cam cleat,** or dropped into the grooved channel of a **clam cleat.**

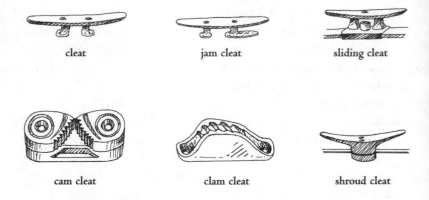

| cleat | jam cleat | sliding cleat |
| cam cleat | clam cleat | shroud cleat |

clevis pin A metal rod that closes a shackle or the jaws of a turnbuckle or other fitting. Some clevis pins are held closed by cotter pins or rings, others by threading (screw pin), others by retractable balls (fast pin, quick-release pin).

clew The after lower corner of a jib, mainsail, or mizzen and one of the two lower corners of a spinnaker.

clinometer An instrument that shows the angle of heel.

clipper bow A bow whose profile sweeps up and forward dramatically.

close Near. To **close the lighthouse** is to approach it. To be **close aboard** or in **close (tight) quarters** is to be very near other objects. **Close-quarters maneuvering** is handling the boat in these situations.

close-hauled, beating, on the wind The point of sail on which the boat sails as close to the wind as possible, with sails trimmed tight.

close-winded Able to sail especially close to the wind.

club 1) A boom. A **club-footed jib** is a jib with a boom. 2) A boat or yacht club. **Club racing** is racing only among the club's fleet, with no outsiders.

close-hauled

CMG, course made good See made good.

coaming A low wall around a cockpit or other deck opening.

coast, coastline, coastal The shore of the land fronting water. **Coastal** (inshore) refers to the coast and the water adjacent to it; the opposite of offshore. **Coastal waters** include salt water near shore. **Coastal (inshore) boating** takes place for a short duration within sight of shore. **Coastal navigation,** see navigate. **Coastal passagemaking,** see passage.

Coast Guard, United States Coast Guard, USCG A military branch, part of the Department of Transportation, that supervises federal boating areas and enforces boating regulations. Its volunteer arm, the **United States Coast Guard Auxiliary (USCGA),** provides courtesy inspections of boats and teaches boating skills in its many flotillas.

Coast Pilot A U.S. government publication providing detailed descriptions of boating areas and harbors.

coating Paint or varnish.

cockbill(ed) See acockbill.

cocked hat In navigation, the area in which three or more bearings cross.

cockpit A recessed area in the deck for the crew.
code flag See flags.
coffee grinder See grind.
COG, course over the ground See made good.

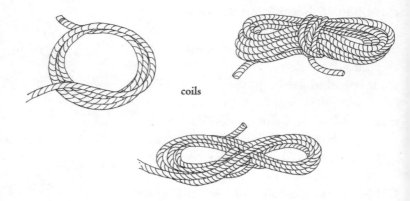

coils

coil To arrange a line in neat, regular loops; they make up a coil.
cold-molded construction Wooden boat construction in which the wood is encapsulated in resin.
collision course, collision situation When a boat is steered toward another boat with a likelihood of colliding, she is on a **collision course**. Both boats then are in a **collision situation,** and one or both must alter course to avoid collision.
colors 1) The yacht ensign or national flag. To **make colors** is to hoist the ensign, to **strike colors** is to lower it. 2) The time of day when the ensign is raised or lowered.
COLREGS See Navigation Rules.
come about, go about To tack.
come up See head up.
commission To prepare a boat for the season. A boat **in commission** is prepared, launched, and ready for use.
committee boat A boat used by officials supervising a race.
commodore A yacht club's highest officer. The next highest is the **vice commodore,** followed by the **rear commodore.**

Because each is assigned a distinctive flag they are called flag officers. The term comes from an historic navy rank just below admiral.

companionway, companion The passageway from the deck or cockpit through a hatch and down steps to the cabin. It may be sealed off by washboards.

COMPASS

A device indicating directions and bearings in compass degrees, of which there are 360, from north through east to south and through west back to north. Degrees are displayed on the **compass card,** as are **the cardinal compass points** (north, east, south, and west). Some compasses also display the **intercardinal compass points** (northeast, southeast, southwest, and northwest). To **box the compass** is to name the compass points. There are several types of compass:

- A **gyrocompass** shows true degrees, which are oriented to the earth's true north.

- The more common **magnetic compass** is oriented to the earth's magnetic field and shows magnetic directions, which usually lie to the side of the corresponding true directions. That difference is called variation. The remainder of this discussion concerns magnetic compasses.

- A **fluxgate compass** is an unusually accurate electronic magnetic compass that can be connected to navigation instruments.

- A **steering compass** is used for steering, a **bearing compass** for taking bearings. A **hand-bearing compass** is a handheld compass for taking bearings. A **telltale compass** is a compass located below, where other members of the crew can keep track of courses steered.

The **compass course** is the course steered **by the compass** (using the compass as a guide). It differs from the course made good (CMG)—the course relative to geography—takes all factors into account, and is displayed by GPS or Loran-C navigation instruments. A **compass bearing** is the direction to an object as read on the compass. To **take (cut) a compass bearing** is to take a bearing.

Compass error is an inaccuracy in a compass due to maladjustment or to **compass deviation,** the effect of metal objects on board. Error can be removed or compensated. A **compass adjuster** is a technician who corrects or compensates compass error. A **compass magnet** is a small magnet that may be placed near the compass to correct compass error.

Navigation devices that refer to compass courses and bearings mimic the compass.

- The **compass rose** on a chart usually shows both true and magnetic directions.

- A **compass protractor** is a navigational plotter with a compass rose that orients it to the chart. See lubber's line and made good.

composite construction Construction of a sail, hull, or other object using different materials, which usually are glued together.

console A structure in a powerboat, supporting the steering wheel, instruments, and engine controls. A **center console** is in the middle of the cockpit. A **split console** is divided by a passageway.

convertible A powerboat that has fishing gear and comfortable accommodations. She is easily converted from a fishing boat to a cruiser.

cordage See rope.

core In boat construction, a light material (usually balsa wood or foam) sandwiched between two layers of fiberglass to stiffen the structure without adding too much weight.

Corinthian Amateur.

corrected time See first, handicap, rating rule.

cotter pin, cotter ring, cotter, cotter key A short wire inserted in an object to secure it, for example in the barrel of a turnbuckle to keep it from rotating and in a clevis pin to hold it in place. A **straight cotter pin** (**cotter key**, split pin) is like a hairpin and has two legs that are spread to hold it in place. A **cotter ring** is circular.

counter The underside of the after overhang (the area of the hull that lies above the water, near the stern). In a **counter stern** the counter extends some distance before it is cut off by the transom.

course, heading 1) The direction in which the boat is steered. To **alter course** is to change direction. To **hold course** is to steer the same direction. To steer **off course** is to not steer the desired course. To steer **on course** is to steer the desired course. The **proper course** is the course that keeps the boat out of danger and provides the most direct route to the destination. 2) The sequence of marks in a race.

course made good, CMG, course over the bottom (ground), COG See made good.

courtesy flag The flag of the host nation, flown in the starboard rigging of a visiting vessel.

cove A small harbor.

cover 1) A fabric placed over the hull or gear (**boat cover, cockpit cover, brightwork cover, winch cover**) or around a sail (**sail cover**) when it is not in use, to protect against water, dirt, and ultraviolet rays. 2) In sailboat racing, to sail between another boat and the wind to slow her down or keep her from passing. See blanket and slam dunk.

cove stripe A decorative stripe running fore and aft on the topside just below the rail.

cowl An air scoop in a ventilator.

CPR, cardiopulmonary resuscitation The technique for manually sustaining breathing and heartbeat in medical emergencies.

CQR Pronounced "secure." A plow anchor.

crack To ease.

cradle A support for a hull out of the water.

craft A generic term for boats as a group, for example **power-craft**. A final "s" is never added; there are no "crafts." The right usage is illustrated by this example: "All **craft** (not 'the crafts') appearing in our Fourth of July nautical parade are advised to fly colorful flags." See small-craft advisory.

crane A strut high on a mast that supports a halyard block or stay.

crank To turn. To **crank a winch** is to turn the winch handle. A boat **cranked down** is heeled far over.

cranky Difficult to steer, unstable.

creep Permanent stretch in sailcloth or other fabric.

crest The top of a wave.

crew Generally, each person in a boat as well as the group as a totality, but often refers to everybody except the skipper or captain. A person can be a **crew** or a **crewmember**.

crew overboard, COB, man overboard, MOB A crewmember who has fallen into the water. **Crew overboard gear** is the emergency equipment used in a **crew overboard rescue**.

cringle An eye in the edge of a sail, used to secure it to a line or shackle.

cross To go in front of another boat.

crossbeam See wing.

crosscut Describes a sail that has horizontal seams. Compare with radial cut.

crosstree The British word for spreader.

crowd on sail To carry as much sail as possible.

crown 1) Upward curvature in a deck. 2) See anchor.

cruise A period of time longer than two days spent sailing between ports and living in a nonracing boat. Compare with weekend.

cruiser, cruising boat A boat with living accommodations in which comfort, seaworthiness, and good stability are more important than speed. Among sailboats, a **cruising boat** or **long-distance cruiser** has moderate to heavy displacement and substantial, comfortable accommodations, and a **cruiser-racer** is comfortable enough for cruising and fast enough for racing. Among powerboats longer than 25 feet, a trawler is boxy and heavy, a **sedan (convertible) cruiser** is lighter and able to plane, and an **express cruiser** (sunbridge) is especially fast and racy looking, without a cabin projecting above the rail.

cruising guide A detailed guide to anchorages, channels, shore facilities, and other items of interest to boaters.

cruising range The distance a boat can cover under power without refueling.

cruising speed The speed under power at which the engine is most efficient.

cuddy See cabin.

Cunningham A sail control line leading through a cringle, or hole, in the lower part of the sail's luff. Thought to have been invented by Briggs Cunningham.

Cup See America's Cup.

current The horizontal motion of water. A **tidal current** is caused by the tide, a **wind-driven current** by the wind. A seiche is a **lake current**. See tide.

curtains Besides the familiar meaning, enclosures around a powerboat's steering area that protect the steerer from the weather.

custom boat, custom design, one-off A boat or design produced uniquely for its owner. Compare with stock boat. A **semicustom boat** is a stock boat with extensive custom features.

cutter See rig.

cycle Refers to the number of strokes that an engine makes. **Two-cycle engines** include many outboard engines. Inboard engines are **four-cycle.**

cyclone 1) A hurricane or other very intense storm, usually in tropical regions. 2) A low-pressure system. An **anticyclone** is a high-pressure system. 3) **Cyclonic winds** rotate counter-clockwise in the Northern Hemisphere, clockwise in the Southern Hemisphere.

Dacron Trademarked type of polyester used in many sails.

daggerboard See centerboard.

dampen To moderate motion.

Danforth A brand name for an anchor. Often used to indicate any lightweight anchor.

danger bearing A bearing or course that marks the limit of safe navigation. To go the wrong side of it is to place the boat at risk.

danger sector See sector.

danger signal Five or more quick blasts on a horn or whistle to alert nearby boats to potential danger.

dangerous semicircle, dangerous quadrant The most risky part of a gale or storm, it is the right front section as the storm advances (the left front section in the Southern Hemisphere).

datum The plane of reference from which the height of the tide and land is reckoned.

davit A small crane on deck, used to hoist a dinghy, anchor, or other object.

daybeacon, beacon, daymark A stake driven into the bottom at the edge of a channel and displaying a placard (**daymark**) with identifying numbers and colors. It takes the place of a buoy as an aid to navigation in very shallow water.

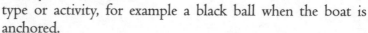
daysailer

daysail To go sailing for a few hours. A **daysailer** is a boat without a cabin (though she may have a cuddy), used for short sails and racing

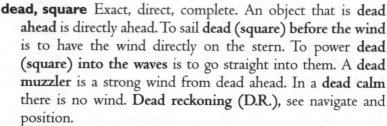

dayshape A signal hung during the day to indicate the vessel's type or activity, for example a black ball when the boat is anchored.

dead, square Exact, direct, complete. An object that is **dead ahead** is directly ahead. To sail **dead (square) before the wind** is to have the wind directly on the stern. To power **dead (square) into the waves** is to go straight into them. A **dead muzzler** is a strong wind from dead ahead. In a **dead calm** there is no wind. **Dead reckoning (D.R.)**, see navigate and position.

dead end To secure an end of a line to a stationary object.

deadhead A mostly submerged log, sometimes used as a mooring buoy.

dead in the water Stopped.

deadlight A port or window that cannot be opened.

deadman's switch Kill switch.

dead reckoning, D.R. See navigate and position.

deadrise The angle of the boat's bottom to the horizontal. A flat bottom has 0 degrees of deadrise. A deep-**V** powerboat hull has about 25 degrees.

deadwood The part of a keel that does not contain ballast.

deck The lid on a boat on which the crew walks and sits. A **decked boat (deck boat)** has a deck, unlike an open boat. The **foredeck** is forward of the cockpit in a powerboat, of the mast in a sailboat. A **deck beam** is a length of wood, fiberglass, or wood supporting the deck. The **side decks** are on both sides. The **afterdeck** is near the stern. A **deck box** is a locker on deck. **Deck gear** consists of cleats, winches, blocks, and other equipment used on deck. A **deck shower** is a fresh-water shower installed on deck or in the cockpit. A **deck-house** is a small cabin on deck. **Deck shoes** have special soles (nonskid soles) that grip a wet, pitching deck. A **deck filler** is an opening in the deck through which a fuel or water tank is filled. A **deck plate** is a small removable hatch in the deck. **Decksweeper,** see low.

deep six To sink.

deep-V See V-bottomed.

deep water Offshore.

delaminate See fiberglass and laminated.

delivery A direct passage to get the boat to a location where she will be met by her owner. Compare with cruise.

departure Leaving port at the beginning of a voyage. The vessel **takes her departure** when she clears land. At the **point of departure** her crew notes the location, the time, the course, and the mileage.

depower To decrease the wind's effect on a sailboat by flattening or reefing a sail, or by changing down to a smaller sail.

depth, water depth The distance from the water's surface to the water's bottom.

depthsounder, echo sounder, sounder, Fathometer, depthfinder An electronic device that indicates the depth of water. A **recording depthsounder** produces a record of depth readings over time.

desalinator See watermaker.

detente A notch in a boat's gear shift that, when engaged, keeps the engine in gear.

deviation Movement of a compass card (measured in degrees west or east) caused by metal or magnetism in the boat. A deviation card displays the amount of deviation at different headings.

diesel A diesel engine, diesel fuel.

differential See Global Positioning System.

dinette An eating area in a boat. A **convertible dinette** can be made into a berth.

dinghy, dink A small, light boat. Compare with pram and tender.

directional stability See stability.

directions Wind directions indicate the direction the wind is blowing from, for example a northwester is a wind from the northwest. All other directions indicate direction toward, for example to steer a course of northwest is to head toward the northwest (or into a northwest wind). See wind.

dirty air Wind affected by another object.

dismasted Suddenly without a mast.

displacement, disp. Technically the amount and weight of water that a hull pushes aside, but generally a boat's weight. It is measured in pounds or in cubic feet, determined by dividing the displacement in pounds by 64. **Light displacement** describes a boat that is relatively lightweight for her length, **heavy displacement** describes a relatively heavy boat, and **moderate displacement** is in the middle. The **displacement/length ratio (D/L ratio)** is a number that indicates a sailboat's displacement relative to her size. The larger the number, the heavier she is. See sail area/displacement ratio.

displacement hull (boat) An especially heavy, full-ended hull or boat. A **semidisplacement hull (semidisplacement boat)** is somewhat lighter.

distance off A boat's distance from a charted object. In the **distance-off navigation technique,** the boat's position is estimated by gauging the distance off from land or a lighthouse's light. That distance is charted as a circle of position. See position.

distance racing See ocean race.

distance run The distance a boat has covered in a known period of time.

distress signal A flare or other visual signal indicating an emergency.

ditch bag See abandon ship.

ditty bag A small bag used to stow and carry a knife, light line, tools, and other boatswain's gear.

diurnal Once daily. Twice daily is **semidiurnal**.

divided rig, split rig See rig.

dividers Calipers (two short metal legs joined at a hinge) used to measure distances on a chart.

dock Technically, the water in which a boat sits when she is tied to a float, pier, or wharf. However, the term usually is used to mean the float, pier, or wharf itself. To **dock** is to pull in to or alongside a dock. **Dockage** is the fee charged for docking, which may be supervised by a **dockmaster**. A **docking line** (**dockline**) is a line used to tie a boat to another object. See breast line, springline. A **dock cart** is a wheelbarrow or wagon used to carry gear down a pier or wharf to the water.

documented A boat registered with the federal government rather than with a state.

dodger A spray shield over and around a hatch.

doghouse A shelter forward of a cockpit or over a hatch.

doldrums A calm area in the middle of an ocean between the trade winds.

dollop A small wave.

dolly A trailer for dinghies, used on launching ramps and in boatyards and not intended to be pulled behind cars.

dolphin Pilings tied together.

dolphin striker See bobstay.

Dorade ventilator See ventilator.

dory A flat-bottomed, double-ended rowing boat originally used as a fishing boat on the Grand Banks.

double To do twice. To **double a peninsula** is to sail around it. To **double up** a line is to rig a backup line. In a **double-bottomed boat**, there is a watertight compartment between the bottom and the cockpit sole.

double-ender, double-ended A boat with a pointed stern. See transom.

doublehanded With a crew of two.

double-headsail rig, double-head rig, cutter rig Having two jibs set simultaneously on two stays. The outer sail (the jib) is set on the headstay; the inner one (the staysail, forestaysail) is set on the forestay.

douse To lower or roll up a sail or awning.

down See head off.

Down East The coast of Maine, especially north and east of Mt. Desert Island.

downflood Water pouring below through a hatch or other opening on deck.

downhaul A line or tackle that pulls down a sail at its tack or holds down a spinnaker pole (also foreguy).

downwind Away from the direction from which the wind is blowing. Opposite of upwind.

D.R. Dead reckoning, dead-reckoning plot. See navigate and position.

draft, dr., draw 1) The boat's extreme depth, from her waterline to her lowest point. A boat has 3 **feet of draft** or **draws 3 feet**; alternatively, **her draft is 3 feet.** 2) The fullness or camber of a sail. See chord.

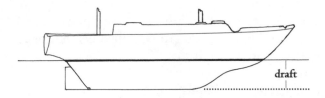

drag 1) Dragging anchor, see anchor. 2) To **drag for** something on the water's bottom is to scrape the bottom with a grapnel hook or net. 3) Concerning sails and appendages, **drag** is resistance to wind or water caused by the object's shape, surface friction, and the process of generating forward force (lift) from air and water flow. Eddies around the leech of a sail or the stern of a boat indicate the presence of drag. Compare with lift and stall.

draw 1) See draft. 2) To design a boat.

dress ship To display flags from bow to stern and aloft in honor of a holiday or an event. A form of flag etiquette.

drift 1) The current's velocity. Compare with set. 2) To not make any speed by power, sail, or oar but rather be pushed by the waves and current. **Drifting conditions** are almost nonexistent winds. A **drifting match** is a race held in drifting conditions. A **drifting jib** or **drifter** (also windseeker) is a light, small sail set in very light wind.

drive 1) To increase speed. When a sailboat **drives off** she heads off and speeds up. To **drive over** another boat means to go by her on her windward side. To **drive (push) a boat hard** is to push her to near her and her crew's limits. **Driving power** is a boat's ability to be pushed hard. 2) **Driveshaft,** the transmission for a boat engine. See V-drive. 3) Steer. The automotive terms **drive** and **driver** have recently come to be used by racing sailors and powerboaters to mean "steer" and "steerer (helmsman)."

drogue A device used to ride out heavy weather and storms. It is a small parachute or other object towed astern. See storm. Compare with sea anchor.

drop To lower.

dry A relative word when used in a boat, it generally means that all the water comes from the sea. A **dry nor'easter** kicks up plenty of spray but provides no rain.

dry rot Rot in wood.

dry store, dry sail To keep a boat out of the water when she is not in use.

dry suit Waterproof one-piece clothing that keeps water out and maintains body heat. Compare with survival suit and wet suit.

dual-purpose boat A racer-cruiser.

---

dual wheels Two steering wheels, one on either side. They allow the steerer to sit far to one side or the other for better visibility forward.

duck 1) To **duck** another boat or **duck astern** of her is to steer behind her, passing astern. 2) To **duck behind** a point of land or breakwater is to go from open water to shelter, where there is protection from wind and waves.

duct A channel for air leading to a ventilator.

DWL, designed waterline See length.

dying Describes a wind that is fading or a sea that is growing flatter.

earing See reef.

ease, ease out, crack, veer out Reduce pressure or tension. To ease a sheet is to let it go a little. To ease the helm is to reduce weather helm. When the wind or sea eases, its force is reduced. Compare with cast off, let fly, let go, pay out, start.

easy Without undue strain. When there is very little weather helm or lee helm the boat has an easy helm. If the boat is not rolling or pitching, she has an easy motion.

ebb, ebb tide See tide.

eddy A circular current. Back eddy, see back.

elapsed time The time it takes for a boat to complete a passage or race. See first, handicap, rating rule.

electronic navigation See navigate.

electronics, electrics All the onboard lights, navigation equipment, and other gear operated by electricity.

emergency gear Backup, safety, and survival equipment used to repair major damage, call for help, abandon ship, rescue a crewmember who has fallen overboard, etc.

encapsulated Contained within. In a fiberglass-encapsulated keel the keel is sheathed with fiberglass.

enclosed Separate or private.

end for end To reverse a docking line, sheet, or other line so the wear is evenly distributed.

ends The bow and stern of a boat. See fine-ended, full-ended.

ensign, yacht ensign, colors The U.S. flag flown from a boat. The U.S. **yacht ensign,** which may be flown only on boats in U.S. waters, displays the fouled anchor (an anchor tangled in a rope) in place of the stars.

entry The bow at and under the water. A **fine entry** is especially sharp, a **full entry** especially broad. See fine-ended and full-ended.

EPIRB, emergency position-indicating radiobeacon A radiobeacon that when activated in an emergency sends a distress signal that can be received by satellites, aircraft, and ships. There are two types of EPIRB: the 406 MHz, which has the longest range and identifies the distressed vessel, and the 121.5 MHz.

estimated position, E.P. See position.

express cruiser A racy-looking, flush-decked, fast power cruiser longer than about 25 feet, for example a Cigarette. She does not have a fly bridge or a cabin rising above the deck. The cabin is a step down from the cockpit. Compare with sedan cruiser.

eye 1) A loop in a line, or the center of an object. An **eye splice** forms a loop at the end of a line or wire. **Eyelet (lacing eye),** see grommet. A **padeye** is a metal loop. 2) The focus or center. The **eye of the wind** is the precise direction of the wind. The **eye of a hurricane** is the center or vortex of the storm. 3) Eyes for seeing. To **keep your weather eye open** is to be an alert lookout. The **eyes of the boat (ship)** are the sides at the bow, just below the deck. In many cultures throughout history the vessel is believed to be a living thing, so human eyes are painted on the bow to allow her to see. This also is where round hawseholes for the anchor rode and docking lines are located on ships and large boats.

F

fair Smooth, easy, comfortable. A **fair wind** is astern, **fair weather** is sunny. A **fair hull** has no bumps or rough spots, and to **fair a hull** is to make it that way.
To **make a lead fair** on a line, arrange it and the block so there is no chafe.

fairlead An eye through which a line is led to keep it from chafing or tangling another line.

fairlead

fairway The middle of a channel.

fake See flake.

fall See tackle.

fall off 1) To tumble down a steep wave. 2) To head off.

family boat, family cruiser A roomy, easy-to-handle boat.

fast Secured. To **make fast** is to secure by cleating, tying, shackling, etc.

fastenings The screws, bolts, etc., holding a boat together.

fast pin See clevis pin.

Fastnet Gale The storm that hit the fleet in the 1979 sailing race from England to Fastnet Rock off Ireland and return. Fifteen sailors died, making this the greatest disaster in the history of pleasure sailing.

fat, heavy Describes a sail that is trimmed too flat or a sailboat that is steered too far off the wind. Compare with light, luff, skinny.

fathom Six feet. The 100-fathom line is the contour in the sea bottom at which the depth is 600 feet. See sound.

Fathometer A brand name for a depthsounder.

favor To ease or help. A **favoring (favorable) wind shift** is a lift or other shift in wind direction that allows a boat to sail closer to her destination.

FCC, Federal Communications Commission The government agency supervising radios and airwaves.

feather 1) See pinch. 2) Turn a propeller or oar so the blade is edge-forward, in order to reduce resistance to water or wind.

federal system See buoy, buoyage.

feeder A slot through which a sail's luff enters a grooved headstay or mast. A **prefeeder** is a device that ensures proper alignment.

feel The pressure on the helm.

fender Padding hung over the topside to protect it from an object alongside. A **fenderboard** is a plank hung outboard of several fenders to improve the protection.

fend off Push off, hold off.

ferrocement A boatbuilding material consisting of mortar laid over wire mesh.

fetch 1) To clear a buoy, point of land, or other object without having to alter course. Also to lay or to make. When **fetching,** the compass course to the object is the layline. 2) The distance over which the wind blows unobstructed.

fiberglass, glass, glassfibre, glass reinforced plastic, GRP, fiberglass reinforced plastic, FRP A construction material composed of layers of glass fibers and cloth laminated together by a glue (resin), often sandwiched around a foam or balsa wood core, and finished on the outside with a hard, glossy surface (gelcoat). These components are laid into a cavity (female mold) that was formed around a full-scale model of the boat (plug). When the components are dry, the pieces are extracted from the mold and assembled with furnishings and gear to make the boat. If water leaks through the gelcoat, the layers of fiberglass and resin may come apart (delaminate) and **fiberglass blisters** (osmotic blisters) may form. The mold and plug are called tooling.

fid See marlinespike.

fiddle A strip of wood secured edgewise on a table to keep small objects from sliding as the boat rolls.

fighting chair See fishing chair.

fill, fill in When a **sail fills,** it catches wind. A calm ends when the **wind fills in.**

fill pipe The inlet for a fuel or water tank.

fine-ended Describes a boat with a narrow bow and stern. Compare with entry and full-ended.

finger pier See pier.

finish 1) The polish on woodwork and other surfaces. A **nicely finished boat** has gleaming paint and varnish. 2) The end of a race.

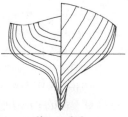

fine-ended

first There are several types of firsts in races. The first boat across the finish line is **first to finish** or **first on elapsed time.** If handicaps are used, the winning boat in the fleet is the one with the lowest corrected time and is **first overall.** The one in each division or class with the lowest corrected time is **first in class.** In a one-design race, the boat that is first to finish is also first overall. See handicap and rating rule.

fish 1) To repair a broken spar by lashing splintlike lengths of wood or metal over the fracture. 2) To lead an internal halyard or messenger through a mast.

fish box An on-deck stowage area for fish that have been caught.

fishhook Besides the usual meaning, a sharp broken strand in a wire.

fishing boat, fishboat A powerboat designed or used for fishing.

fishing chair, fighting chair A chair, often equipped with a restraining belt or harness, used by fishermen when catching and fighting fish.

fit out To prepare a boat for use.

fitted Permanently installed, for example a **fitted bilge pump**.

fitting A cleat, fairlead, or other small piece of gear.

fix In navigation a **fix** is the most reliable calculation and plot of a boat's position. In coastal navigation, a **running fix** based on one bearing is carried forward from a previous fix. See navigate.

fixed Permanent. A **fixed light** on a buoy or lighthouse is always lit at night and in poor visibility. Compare with flashing.

flags Official and **nonofficial flags** are flown to communicate information or simply for the fun of it. They often are hoisted on light lines called **flag halyards**. **Code flags** are official flags representing letters, numbers, and phrases under the International Code of Signals. Pleasure boats also fly flags that identify the owners and their clubs. A **flagstaff** is short spar on which flags are flown. **Flag etiquette** is the name for the rules and customs that govern the display of flags on and near boats. See burgee, dress ship, ensign, pig stick, and private signal. **Flag officer,** see commodore.

flake, fake To coil a line or fold a sail so it will run out easily.

flare, pyrotechnics 1) A highly visible distress signal that signals for help **(red flare)** or to gain the attention of nearby boats **(white flare)**. Flares are fired from small **flare guns,** dropped by parachute from a rocket, or handheld. 2) The outward sweep of a boat's side near the deck, generally near the bow, to direct spray outboard.

flashing Describes a light on a buoy or lighthouse that automatically turns on and off at regular intervals. Compare with fixed.

flat 1) Describes a boat that is not heeling or rolling. 2)

Describes a sail with very little draft (camber). To **flatten a sail** is to pull all its sail controls tight. 3) See calm.

flat-bottomed Describes a boat with a flat or nearly flat bottom with no rocker. Compare with round-bottomed and V-bottomed.

flat-out, serious Highly specialized. A **flat-out (serious) sportfisherman** is a boat designed and used only for that purpose.

flats boat An outboard engine-driven powerboat around 16 feet long, used for fishing in shallow water.

flattening reef See reef.

fleet A particular group of boats, for example **sportfishing fleet, yacht club fleet.**

float, flotation An object that provides buoyancy to keep another object afloat. A **float** is a platform on the water for supporting people, a small buoy supporting an anchor rode at a mooring, or the outside hull of a trimaran. A **float coat** is a parka with enough buoyancy to support the wearer in the water. A **personal flotation device (PFD)** provides buoyancy for an individual. See buoyancy and PFD.

float plan The written, planned itinerary for a cruise, fishing trip, or other time spent afloat. A copy is left ashore with a reliable person who could notify the Coast Guard or other authorities should the boat be overdue.

float switch See bilge.

flog When a sail or line flaps wildly.

flood, flood tide The rising or incoming tide.

floor Athwartships structural support inside the boat's bottom.

floorboards The platforms over the bilge.

flopper-stopper, paravane A device hung alongside in the water from a powerboat's outrigger, to limit rolling.

flotsam Wreckage debris in the water. Compare with jetsam.

flukes See anchor.

fluky Describes a light, shifty wind.

flush deck, raised deck A flat or slightly rounded deck with no cabin protruding.

fluxgate compass See compass.

fly Abbreviation for **masthead fly,** a wind indicator at the top of the mast.

fly bridge, flying bridge See bridge.

fog Condensed water vapor near the water or land that causes poor visibility. Vessels and lighthouses make **fog signals** on their **foghorns.**

foil A rudder or other appendage or sail shaped like an airplane wing. A **hydrofoil** is a horizontal foil on a strut under the hull; the hull lifts out of the water and the boat rides on her foils at high speed.

following From astern, for example **following sea, following wind.** Compare with head.

foot 1) The bottom edge of a sail. A **foot line (foot cord)** is a light line sewn into the foot that can be adjusted to shape the sail. 2) To **foot** is to sail fairly close-hauled without pointing as high as possible, in order to maximize speed. See full.

Force A category in the Beaufort Scale.

FORE, FORWARD

At, near, or toward the bow. Compare with aft, after. To **go forward** is to walk toward the bow. **Forward of the beam** is the area of the boat between abeam and ahead. **Fore and aft** is running from bow to stern, for example in a **fore-and-aft rig** the sails line up with the boat instead of athwartships, as in the square rig.

The words identify equipment by location:

- The **foredeck** is the front part of the deck. The **forebody** is the boat's bottom and sides near the bow. The **forefoot** is the forwardmost part of the underbody, or the area under water.

- The **forward cabin** (stateroom) is the sleeping cabin near

the bow. The **forecastle** (pronounced "focs'l") or **forepeak**
is a stowage compartment in
the very forward part of the
boat.

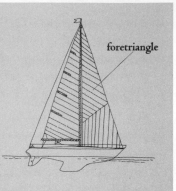

foretriangle

- The **forestay** is a stay running
from the forward deck to partway up the mast, and a
forestaysail is set on the
forestay. The **foretriangle** is the
area in which jibs are set, over the foredeck and between the
mast and the headstay. The **foremast** is the forward mast on
a schooner. The **foreguy** is a line holding the spinnaker pole
down the leads to the foredeck.

forehandedness Anticipation of problems and planning for
emergencies.

forereach To sail slowly almost into the wind.

foresail Pronounced "fore-*sul*." 1) British term for jib. 2) In a
schooner, a small sail set between the two masts.

forestaysail See staysail.

forgiving Describes a boat that is tolerant of her steerer's mis-
takes. She will not readily capsize or be hard to steer.

foul 1) Nasty. **Foul weather** is unpleasant, wet weather. 2) To
entangle. When a line is **fouled on a cleat,** it is wrapped
around it. 3) To violate a racing rule.

foul-weather gear, slicker, oilers, oilies Waterproof clothing.
Often specified by type, for example **foul-weather jacket,
slicker pants.**

found Furnished, equipped. A **well-found boat** is thoroughly
equipped.

founder To swamp or sink.

four-stroke A four-cycle outboard motor.

fractional rig See rig.

frame Athwartships structural support for the hull, running up the boat's sides from the bilge.

free, freeing 1) **Sailing free** is sailing on a broad reach or a run. 2) A **freeing wind** is one that shifts aft.

freeboard The height of the topsides.

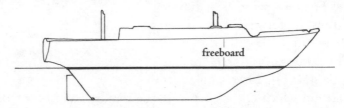

freeboard

freewheel To spin without effect. A **freewheeling propeller** rotates without providing propulsion.

freshen A **freshening wind** is a wind whose speed is increasing. A boat **freshens her wind** by heading up from a run to a reach in order to increase her apparent wind.

fresh wind Wind of 16 to 22 knots.

front The front edge of an arriving weather system, heralding a change of wind and weather.

frostbite To sail during the cold months.

FRP, fiberglass reinforced plastic See fiberglass.

full Describes a sail that is not luffing. Compare with fat and luff. **Full and by** is sailing with sails full.

full-ended Describes a boat with a wide bow and stern. If only the bow is wide, she is bluff-bowed. Compare with entry and fine-ended.

full-ended

full sail With all sails set and not reefed. A boat **under full sail** is sailing with all sails set.

furl To get a sail out of the way by folding it on a boom or rolling it up on a **roller furler.**

gaff

gadget A small, specialized piece of gear. See gilhickey.

gaff 1) The spar aloft on the traditional four-sided **gaff rig**. See rig. 2) A pole with a sharp hook used to retrieve fish from the water.

gale Wind speed of 34 to 47 knots.

galley A boat's kitchen. A **galley strap** is a length of webbing that holds the cook in the galley as the boat heels.

gallows frame, gallows A permanently installed support for the main boom. Compare with boom (boom crutch).

gam To tell sea stories, or a session of storytelling.

gangway, boarding gate An opening in the lifelines or rail, or a ramp that facilitates boarding a boat or a pier.

gantline A sturdy line rigged to the top of the mainmast and used to haul gear or a crewmember in the boatswain's chair aloft when the main halyard is unavailable. Except in emergencies, it is not used to hoist sails. Compare with halyard.

garboard The boat's bottom near the keel.

gas Gasoline or cooking fuel.

gasket A sail stop, a strap or line used to secure a furled sail.

gate valve See seacock.

gear Boating equipment and clothing small and portable enough to be removed from the boat. While a mast and a tuna tower are not gear, a masthead fly and a fishing rod are. **Foul-weather gear** is clothing specific to boating. **Fishing gear** consists of the equipment needed for fishing.

gelcoat See fiberglass.

generator A device for generating electricity. It may be an engine (also called a genset), a propeller in the air (**wind generator**), a propeller towed astern, or a solar panel that converts solar rays to energy.

Gennaker A trademarked name ("genoa" plus "spinnaker") for a type of asymmetrical or cruising spinnaker.

genoa, genny A large overlapping jib, reportedly first publicly used off Genoa, Italy.

genset An engine-powered generator.

gilguy A light line holding a halyard away from a mast to prevent it from clanging.

genoa

gilhickey A makeshift, otherwise unnamed gadget.

gimbal A support for a compass, table, or other object that automatically keeps it level as the boat heels and rolls. The main eating table in a sailboat may be a **gimbaled table** (swing table).

give Stretch or bend.

give way 1) Change position. When a boat alters course to allow another vessel to pass she **gives way**. Under the Navigation Rules (rules of the road), the **give-way vessel** (formerly burdened vessel) is obligated to alter course when two or more vessels are near each other in order to avoid collisions. Compare with stand on. 2) When gear **gives way** it breaks.

glass 1) Fiberglass. 2) **The glass** is the barometer.

Global Maritime Distress and Safety System An international electronic alert system.

Global Positioning System, GPS, satnav An electronic navigation instrument, using information from satellites, that computes and displays the boat's position and information about her course and speed made good. Satnav was the first of these systems. **Differential GPS** is the most accurate. See selective availability (S.A.).

GMT, Greenwich Mean Time, Zulu The time at the Greenwich meridian, or zero degrees longitude.

go about, come about To tack.

gold plater A luxurious boat.

gong, gong buoy See buoy, buoyage.

gooseneck The fitting securing the boom to the mast. A **sliding gooseneck** slides on a track on the mast.

goosewing jibe See jibe.

government mark A channel marker or other buoy set by the Coast Guard or other government agency to serve as an aid to navigation.

GPS Global Positioning System.

grab bag See abandon ship.

grabrail A handhold.

granny A mistied square knot. It will slip.

grapnel anchor, grapnel hook A light, multipronged hook used as a lunch hook or to drag for objects. See anchor.

great circle route The shortest route between two distant points on the globe. This rhumb line is shown as a straight line on a globe or on a gnomic projection chart, but on a Mercator projection chart it is a curve. Under way, the boat makes a series of small course changes in order to stay on the route.

Greenwich meridian, Greenwich Mean Time, GMT See prime meridian and Zulu.

grind, grinder To **grind a winch** is to turn its handle. A **grinder** is a crewmember who grinds. A **coffee grinder (grinder)** is a winch operated by a standing crewmember.

grommet, lacing eye, eyelet A small metal ring inserted in a sail, boat cover, or other cloth. Smaller and lighter than a cringle, it is used by reef points or tie-down lines.

grooved (slotted) headstay, grooved (slotted) mast A groove in the aft side of a headstay or mast into which a sail's boltrope or slugs are fed. A **double-grooved headstay** allows a new jib to be set before the old one is lowered.

"gross tonnage rule" An unofficial safety advisory that suggests that smaller vessels, regardless of their rights under the formal Navigation Rules, should always stay clear of big ones.

ground Run aground.

groundswell Long waves that run almost continuously due to prevailing winds. Compare with swell.

ground system Protection in a boat, intended to prevent damage caused by a lightning strike.

ground tackle The anchor, its rode, and related equipment.

guardrails The pulpit.

gudgeon See pintle.

gunkhole, mud hole A creek, cove, marsh, or other shallow corner in the shore. **Gunk** means mud. To **gunkhole** or go **gunkholing** is to explore such places in a boat, although sometimes these terms are used to mean going ashore to explore on foot.

gunwale Pronounced "gunnel." See rail.

gust A sudden, strong puff of wind.

guy A line used to position a spinnaker pole or other spar. The **afterguy** controls a spinnaker pole's fore-and-aft position, the **foreguy** holds it down. To **guy (guy back)** the pole is to pull on the afterguy.

gybe See jibe, gybe.

hail To call out to a boat, addressing her by her name and her port. A **loudhailer (hailer)** is an electricity-amplified megaphone.

hailing port, home port 1) The place where a boat usually is docked or moored. 2) The name of the town or port painted on the transom.

halyard A wire or line that pulls up, holds up, and lowers a sail or flag. An **internal halyard** is led partly inside the mast, an **external halyard** is entirely outside it. A **halyard lock** is a mechanical device that holds a sail aloft, sometimes by a hook at the masthead. **Halyard stopper,** see lock-off.

hand 1) Side. The **starboard hand** is the starboard side, the **port hand** the port side. 2) A crewmember. A **deckhand** is assigned to handle docking lines, anchors, and other lines and gear. A **foredeck hand** is assigned to handle jibs, spinnakers, and other sails and gear forward of the mast. A **paid hand** is a professional crew. 3) A human hand. **Hand signal.** A visual signal made when verbal commands are inaudible. The saying **"one hand for yourself, one for the boat"** means that each person is responsible for her or his individual safety while also steering, crewing, and otherwise managing the boat.

4) To lower. To **hand a sail** is to lower the sail. See forehandedness.

hand-bearing compass See compass.

handheld Small enough to be held when in operation, for example a **handheld radio**.

handhold, handrail, grabrail, security rail A rail, bar, indentation, or strap that provides support when the boat heels or pitches.

handicap An attempt to equalize boats of different size in a race by making time corrections. A **handicap system** assigns corrections based on predictions of a boat's speed and the length of the course. One system is the **Performance Handicap Racing Fleet (PHRF)**. See first. Compare with rating rule.

handle 1) To **handle a boat** or a task is to manage it in a seamanlike and seaworthy way. **Small-boat handling** is the art and science of handling vessels shorter than about 40 feet, while **ship handling** concerns ships and other vessels longer than about 100 feet. 2) Winch handle.

handsomely In a skillful, seamanlike manner.

handy 1) Describes an especially useful person or maneuverable boat. 2) Close at hand.

handy billy See tackle.

hank A metal or plastic hook that secures a jib to a stay. A **snaphank** (snaphook) is opened by pushing its retaining pin sideways, a **piston hank** by pulling the pin out. To **hank on** a jib is to hook it to its stay in preparation for hoisting.

harbormaster, port captain The official who enforces port regulations and supervises mooring, docking, etc.

hard 1) All the way. To put the helm **hard over** is to push or turn it as far as possible. When the helm is **hard up**, the boat heads off; when **hard down**, she heads up. **"Hard alee"** ("lee-oh") is the steerer's report that the helm is hard down and the boat is tacking. To be **hard aground** is to be completely stuck on the water's bottom. 2) **The hard** is the water's bottom when exposed at low tide. 3) A sail that is **hard** is full, or trimmed correctly. Compare with soft.

hard chance A beat to windward in heavy weather.

harden 1) To **harden up** is to head up. 2) To **harden a sail** is to trim it until it stops luffing; a sail is full when it is **hard**.

hardtop A fiberglass or wooden cover over the helm to protect the steerer. Compare with T-top.

hardware Small items of equipment.

hatch An opening in a deck. It is covered by a **hatch cover,** and the opening may be closed by a **hatchboard** (washboard, slat).

haul 1) To pull. The **hauling part of a tackle** is its fall. To **haul (haul out)** a boat is to lift her out of the water. See **downhaul** and **outhaul.** 2) See veer.

hawse, hawsepipe 1) A hole in the bow for the anchor rode. A **hawser** is an especially large docking or towing line. 2) A hole in a rail or deck for a docking line.

hazard to navigation A shallow area, rock, drifting boat, or other potentially dangerous object.

head 1) The bow. A **head sea** is a series of waves from ahead. A **head wind** is wind from ahead. 2) A boat's toilet or toilet room, both of which traditionally were located in the bow. An **enclosed head** is a toilet with a door.

headboard Reinforcement at the head of a mainsail.

header A wind shift that forces the steerer of a sailboat to head off in order to keep the sails full. Compare with lift.

heading The course steered.

head off, head down, bear away, bear off, come off, drive off, fall off, pay off, round off Change course downwind, or away from the wind's direction.

headroom The interior height of a cabin. **Standing headroom** permits most people to stand erect, **sitting headroom** permits most people to sit comfortably.

heads See bollards.

headsail Pronounced "head-*sul.*" Jib.

headstay, jibstay See stay.

head to wind Steering directly into the wind. See no-go zone.

head up, harden up, come up, round up, freshen your wind, sharpen up, sharpen your wind Change course upwind, or toward the wind's direction.

headway A boat's forward motion. Compare with sternway.

heat up, heat it up To head up from a run to a reach.

heave To throw.

heave-to To carry a minimum of sail or power so the boat can steer herself while she rides comfortably. With a sailboat the wind is about 60 degrees off the bow, the mainsail may be reefed, and the jib may be backed. This is a storm tactic and a simple way to slow a boat. **Hove-to** describes a boat engaged in this maneuver and also is the past tense of **heave-to**. Sometimes used to mean stop the boat. See Rod-stop.

heavily built Constructed with heavy components. Compare with lightly built.

heaving line, throw rope A light line that can be easily thrown to another boat or to a swimmer needing rescue. A **throw bag** is a heaving line contained in a small bag that is thrown in order to add force.

heavy 1) Forceful. **Heavy air (heavy wind, heavy breeze)** is a strong wind (22 knots or higher), **heavy seas** are large waves, and **heavy weather** includes both. See rage. 2) Weighty. A **heavy-displacement boat** weighs a great deal for her length. 3) A sail is described as **heavy** when it is trimmed too far. See fat; compare with light.

heel 1) Tipping caused by the wind. 2) The bottom of a mast; see step.

helm 1) The steering wheel or tiller. 2) The steerer or **helmsman**. 3) The pull on the wheel or tiller. **Weather helm** (sometimes simply **helm**) is the tendency to round up into the wind when the tiller or wheel is released. **Lee helm** is the tendency to head off. See balance.

helmsman, helmsperson The steerer.

her See boat names.

high Above. A **high-cut jib**'s clew is well above the deck. To steer **high of course** is to steer above course. The **high side** is the windward side of a heeling boat. Compare with low.

high performance See performance.

high seas Far out in an ocean or sea.

high-water mark The line of debris, weed, or erosion on the shore or a pier at the average high-water level.

hike To lean out to windward to counteract a sailboat's heel. The British term is sit out. To **hike a boat flat** is to eliminate all heel by hiking. A **hiking strap** is a strap that restrains the hiking sailor's feet and legs. A **hiking stick** (tiller extension) is an extension on the tiller, allowing the helmsman to hike. **Hike** sometimes means heel.

hike

hitch 1) See knot. 2) **Trailer hitch,** see trailer.

Hobie Cat A brand of small catamarans designed originally by Hobie Alter.

hockey puck A small hand-bearing compass. The early ones were shaped like hockey pucks.

hockle A kink in a line.

hogged Describes a boat whose bow and stern have drooped.

hoist 1) Pull up a sail by its halyard. 2) The length of a sail's luff.

holding ground The water's bottom in which a boat is anchored. **Good holding ground** provides a strong bite for the anchor flukes, **poor holding ground** is rocky, weedy, or mushy.

holding power The relative ability of the ground tackle to grab and hold the bottom.

holding tank A container for storage of sewage waste. See marine sanitation device.

hole A small patch of light wind. When a sailboat **falls into a**

hole she is in a lull.

home port See hailing port.

hook 1) Slang for anchor. 2) **Snaphook,** see hank.

hoop See mast.

horn signal See sound signal.

horseshoe, horseshoe buoy A life ring–type PFD (personal flotation device) shaped like a horseshoe. The open end facilitates entry in the water.

hot bunks Berths constantly in use by crewmembers as watches change during an ocean passage.

hounds The point on the mast where the jib's halyard sheave is located.

house See trunk.

houseboat A boxy flat-bottomed or pontoon boat usually used in lakes and rivers.

hovercraft A boat, propelled by a fan-type device, that skims across the water and weeds.

hove-to See heave-to.

hull The area of a boat that lies between the deck and the keel. The **hull-to-deck joint** is the connection between the hull's sides and the deck at the rail. **Hull speed** is the theoretical highest speed that a **displacement hull (nonplaning hull)** can reach because it must plow through the water. See speed. A boat that is **hull-down** is far enough away so her hull is hidden behind the earth's curvature.

hunt, hunt down To steer toward another boat in order to force her to alter course.

hurricane The worst possible weather, with winds in excess of 64 knots and 45-foot waves at sea. **Hurricane alert (hurricane watch, hurricane warning),** see weather alert.

hydraulic system, hydraulics A device that applies energy through a highly pressurized reservoir of light oil. Some engines have **hydraulic drives** in place of mechanical transmissions. In **hydraulic steering,** the rudder is turned using a hydraulic system.

hydrodynamics The study of the flow of liquids. Compare with aerodynamics.

hydrofoil A skilike device under a hull. When the boat is going fast enough, the hull lifts out of the water and rides on its hydrofoils at high speeds. Used mainly on powerboats.

hydroplane A very high speed, flat-bottomed racing powerboat that skims across the water.

hyperthermia Dangerous rise of body heat.

hypothermia Dangerous loss of body heat.

ice bag The original name of today's tote bag, which was used to carry ice to the boat.

iceboat A sailboat on ice skates.

ICW Intracoastal Waterway.

impeller A small paddlewheel in a through-hull that pushes water into an engine's cooling system or senses a boat's speed.

in A person **sails in a boat,** not on her.

inboard Toward the center of the boat from the side. An **inboard engine** is inside the hull. Compare with outboard.

inboard/outboard drive, I/O, outdrive, stern drive A powerboat propulsion system that combines an inboard motor in the boat and an outboard driveshaft and propeller behind the transom.

inflatable Capable of being inflated. Describes or refers to a PFD, life raft, dinghy, or other floating object whose buoyancy is provided by air inserted by a carbon dioxide cartridge. An **automatic inflatable** inflates when it goes into the water. The inflation system in a **manual inflatable** is triggered by hand. A **hard-bottomed inflatable dinghy** has a small fiberglass hull.

-ing Added to the name of a compass cardinal point to indicate distance made good in a direction. **Easting** is distance made good to the east.

in irons, in stays Headed directly into the wind with no headway.

initial stability See stability.

inland Away from the ocean. **Inland waters** are lakes and rivers. **Inland waterway,** see Intracoastal Waterway.

Inland Navigational Rules See Navigation Rules.

inlet A narrow opening in a shoreline that provides access to a harbor.

inshore, near shore Coastal.

instruments Electronic engine, speed, depth, navigation, and other indicators.

intent-agreement signal See sound signal.

intercardinal points See compass.

interior The cabins.

intermediates See stay.

international code Signal flags for letters and numbers.

International Maritime Organization, IMO An organization that sets standards for maritime safety.

International Measurement System, IMS See rating rule.

International Rules of the Road, COLREGS See Navigation Rules.

International Sailing Federation, ISF The international organization that governs sailboat racing. Formerly the International Yacht Racing Union (IYRU).

interval The amount of time between flashes of a buoy's or lighthouse's light.

Intracoastal Waterway, ICW, inland waterway A protected channel running along the U.S. Atlantic and Gulf coasts.

inverter A device that changes 12-, 24-, or 32-volt direct current (D.C.) to 120-volt alternating current (A.C.). Compare with transformer.

islet A small island.

it See boat names.

jack A prefix meaning "handy" or "useful" that sometimes is applied to new gear that does not yet have a distinctive name of its own.

jackline A safety line or wire running along the deck, cabin, or cockpit to which the crew hooks safety harness tethers.

jackstay 1) Babystay. 2) British term for jackline.

jaws The sides of a U-shaped opening in a fitting, such as a shackle, intended to be secured to another object, such as a padeye. The jaws are fitted over the object, then closed and secured to it with a clevis pin. Jaws are also found in toggles, in the ends of turnbuckles, and in the gaff in a gaff sailboat rig.

jet boat A boat with a jet-drive engine that provides propulsion not through a propeller but by pushing water. **Jet Ski,** see personal watercraft.

jetsam Goods thrown from a disabled vessel to lighten her. Compare with flotsam.

jetty Breakwater.

Jib, Headsail

Sometimes foresail. **Jib** rhymes with "bib." A sail set between the forwardmost mast and the headstay. All jibs are trimmed using a **jibsheet,** a line that passes through a block on deck (**jib lead**).

Many sailboats have several jibs of different sizes, shapes, and purposes.

- Some jibs in a sail inventory are identified by their size relative to the foretriangle. A 100 **percent jib** (sometimes **working jib**) fills the foretriangle, as does a **blade jib** (**blade**). Jibs identified as larger than 100 percent extend aft of the mast, for example 130 percent, 150 percent. Because they overlap the mast they are called **overlapping jibs** (lappers). Often jibs are called by their relative size, with the largest the **number 1 jib** and the smallest usually the **number 4 jib.**

  - A **genoa jib** (genoa, genny) is a large overlapping jib.

  - Some jibs are known by their function, for example **reaching jib, storm jib** (spitfire).

A **jib boom** is a boom for a jib. A forestaysail (staysail) is set partway between the mast and headstay on the forestay (inner headstay). A **jib topsail** (**jib top**) is set high on the headstay.

jibe, gybe Rhymes with "tribe." "Jibe" is used in America, "gybe" in other parts of the world. To change tacks by heading off until the sails swing across the boat. In a **flying jibe** the sails bang across dangerously; this may cause a **goosewing jibe,** where the boom or a batten hangs up on a stay. **"Jibe-ho"** is the command for a jibe.

jib-headed rig See rig.

jibstay, headstay See stay.

jig A small block and tackle.

jigger See mizzen, jigger.

jockey pole See reaching strut.

jog, jog along To move along slowly and comfortably.

judge, jury See racing rules.

jumper strut, jumpers A short rod extending forward from the mast. The **jumper stay** leads over it and gives fore-and-aft support to the upper mast. See stay.

junior program A boating instruction course for children.

jury rig An expedient repair, or to make such a repair.

K

kedge See anchor, hook.
kedge off To pull a grounded boat into navigable water using
   an anchor.

KEEL

A fin under a sailboat's hull providing weight for stability and
lateral resistance to leeway. It consists largely of ballast. Unlike
centerboards, most keels are fixed in place and not retractable
(the exception is the **lifting keel**). A **keel boat** is any boat with
a keel. A **keel-centerboarder** is a keel boat that also has a centerboard. There are several types of keel:

- A **fin keel** is small and not attached to the rudder.

- A **continuous (full-length) keel** runs much of the length
of the underbody and is attached to the rudder.

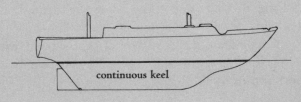

continuous keel

- A **winged** (**wing**) **keel** has short horizontal fins that improve water flow.

- A **bulb keel** has a large bulb at its bottom to place the ballast low.

- **Twin** (**bilge**) **keels** come in a pair, with one short keel on either side of the boat's bottom.

- A **canting keel** swings sideways as the boat heels so it remains vertical and provides best performance.

keep clear To stay safely away from another boat or object.

ketch See rig.

Kevlar Brand name for the low-stretch fabric aramid. Used in sails, line, and boat construction.

kicker A very small outboard motor. See troll.

kicking strap, kicker British words for boom vang.

kill switch, kill lanyard, deadman's switch A device that automatically shuts off an engine if the steerer falls overboard.

kinetics In sailboat racing, shifting the crew's weight to increase the boat's speed.

kite Spinnaker. A **shy kite** is a small spinnaker set on a close reach.

knee A triangular wooden or metal plate inside the hull that connects structural members, for example a deck beam with a frame.

knock To be adversely affected by the wind or a wave. A **knock** is a header. A boat that is **knocked down** or **knocked flat** or suffers a **knockdown** is suddenly heeled dangerously far.

knockabout A sailboat without a bowsprit.

knot 1) Turns in a line that form a loop or secure the line to another line or object. Technically there are three types of knot: the loop knot, which makes loops; the bend, which ties lines together; and the hitch, which secures a line to an anchor, bitt, or other object. These terms are used inconsis-

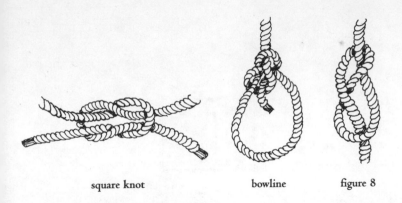

square knot   bowline   figure 8

tently, however, and **knot** generally refers to all three. 2) Speed of 1 nautical mile (6,076 feet, or 1.15 statute miles) per hour. A **10-knot wind** is blowing 11.5 statute miles per hour. A **knotmeter** is a boat's speedometer. 3) It is unusual, but technically not wrong, to say **"a 10-knot-per-hour wind."** This is because under an old definition, a **knot** is a nautical mile.

laboring Describes a boat whose progress is slow and uncomfortable.

lake breeze See sea breeze.

laminated Different materials glued together, for example layers of fiberglass in a hull and **polyester-Mylar sailcloth laminate**. To **delaminate** is to come unglued. See composite construction and fiberglass.

land breeze, shore breeze, offshore wind Wind blowing from the land over the water. Compare with sea breeze.

landfall First sight of land during a passage. Boats **make a landfall** when land is first sighted.

landlubber Somebody who knows little about the sea and boats and does things in a **landlubberly** way.

lane Route. A **shipping lane** is a channel often used by big ships and is therefore risky for pleasure boats.

lanyard A short length of light line that secures an object.

lapper An overlapping jib. See jib.

lash To secure using rope.

lateen rig See rig.

lateral buoyage system, federal system See buoy, buoyage.

lateral resistance See appendage.

latitude The angular distance north or south of the equator, expressed in degrees and minutes. On a chart or map, **parallels of latitude** run west to east. Compare with longitude.

launch 1) To put a boat in the water. A **launching ramp** is a sloping part of the shore where a trailerable boat may be launched by pushing the trailer into the water. 2) A **launch** also is a powerboat that ferries people from shore to boats; also water taxi.

lay, laid 1) Prepare, arrange. To **lay up** is to prepare a boat for storage at the end of the boating season. To **lay out gear** is to prepare equipment for use. A **layout** is an arrangement of a boat's cabins and equipment. The **layup** is the order in which the elements of fiberglass are arranged. 2) **Lay a buoy** and **layline**, see fetch. 3) A **lay day** is a day off from boating. 4) **Laid rope**, see rope.

lazarette A stowage area under a hatch in the afterdeck.

lazy Untensioned, temporarily not in use. When two sheets or guys are attached to a sail, the **lazy sheet** or **lazy guy** is the one that does not have tension on it. The other is the loaded one.

lazyjacks Several interconnected lines running from partway up the mast to partway along the boom to form a web that restrains the sail when it is lowered.

lead 1) When pronounced "leed," to direct or reeve a line through a block or eye. It also is the block itself; a **jib lead** is a block for the jibsheet. 2) When pronounced "led," the **lead (lead line)** is a line with a weight on the end, used to measure water depth manually.

leak Undesired entry of water into a boat or of air out of a container.

leave To pass. To **leave a buoy to port** is to steer so the buoy is on the boat's port side.

leeboard A retractable fin in the water that is hung not from the centerline (as a centerboard is) but outboard near the rail. Leeboards usually come in pairs, one on each side.

leech Sometimes misspelled "leach." The after or back edge of a sail. A **tight leech** is straight, a **hooked (cupped) leech** curves abruptly, and a **loose (floppy) leech** shakes. A **leech line (leech cord)** sewn into the leech can be adjusted to shape the sail.

leecloth, bunkboard A length of fabric or wood serving as a temporary side of a bunk to keep the sleeper from falling out as the boat heels.

leeward, lee Leeward is pronounced "loo-ward"; **lee** is pronounced as spelled. Compare with windward. The **leeward (lee) side (rail, bow)** are on the side that is not closest to the wind. A **lee shore** is land onto which the wind is blowing from the water. **Leeward (lee) helm,** see helm. **"Lee-oh"** is the British equivalent of **"hard alee"**—the command when tacking. To **lee bow** another boat is to place your boat on her leeward bow; your position is the **safe leeward position.**

leeway Sideslippage downwind. When a boat **makes leeway** she slides to leeward while also making progress ahead.

leg A section of a cruise, passage, or race course defined by intermediate stops or turning marks.

length Every boat has two lengths. The **length overall (overall length, LOA)** is the distance on deck from stem to stern—the tip of the bow to the end of the stern (the bowsprit and boomkin are not included). The **waterline length (length on the waterline, LWL; designed waterline length, DWL)** is the straight-line distance between the boat's two extreme points at the water's surface. Length sometimes is an abbreviation for **boat length.**

let fly, loose, lose To instantly free a line so it can run out, often in the context of an emergency. Compare with cast off, ease, let go, let out, pay out.

let go To drop the anchor.

let out To ease a sheet a short distance. Compare with pay out and let fly, lose.

level racing, class racing Competition between sailboats of the same class or rating.

license See certificate and operator's license.

lie ahull See ahull.

life belt PFD (personal flotation device) or safety harness.

life harness Safety harness.

life jacket, life vest, life preserver, life ring See PFD (personal flotation device).

lifeline A wire encircling the deck above the rail, supported by metal posts (stanchions), to help keep the crew on deck. **Double lifelines** have two wires, one above the other.

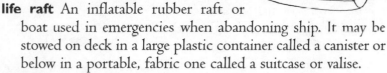

lifelines

life raft An inflatable rubber raft or boat used in emergencies when abandoning ship. It may be stowed on deck in a large plastic container called a canister or below in a portable, fabric one called a suitcase or valise.

liferails See pulpit.

Lifesling, Seattle sling The Lifesling is a patented device for recovering someone who has fallen overboard. Because it was invented in Seattle, Washington, it sometimes is called the **Seattle sling.**

lift 1) A wind shift that allows a sailboat to head up. Compare with header. 2) **Topping lift.** 3) The aerodynamic or hydrodynamic force generated as wind or water passes over a sail, keel, centerboard, or rudder. Compare with drag and stall.

light 1) Weight or force. A **lightly built boat** is constructed with lightweight components. See displacement and sail. A **light wind (light air, light breeze)** is less than 8 knots. A sail that is **light** is luffing. Compare with heavy. 2) Illumination. Many buoys and lighthouses have fixed or blinking electric lights with colors, patterns, and intervals called characteristics and phase characteristics, which are recorded in a publication, the *Light List.* For **boat lights,** see navigation lights.

lighthouse An aid to navigation that is a conspicuous building displaying a light and often sounding a horn in poor visibility.

lightstick A small container of chemicals that when broken sheds a bright light.

limber hole A small hole inside a boat that permits water to flow to the deepest part of the bilge, where the bilge pump's intake is located.

line 1) A length of rope used for a particular purpose (the only piece of rope on a boat is the boltrope). **Light line** is utility line larger than string but smaller than sheets or halyards. A line has three parts: the bitter end (the very end), the standing part (the inactive part), and the bight (the central or curved part in use between the bitter end and standing part). To **reeve a line** is to lead it through a block. 2) A race begins at the **starting (start) line** and ends at the **finishing (finish) line**.

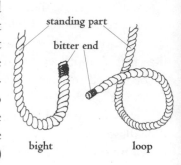

standing part

bitter end

bight   loop

line honors A distinction or prize going to the first boat to finish a race.

line of position, LOP position.

line of sight The distance a person can see in clear visibility—about 5 miles from the deck of a boat.

line stopper See lock-off.

liner A layer of material on the inside of the boat that prevents condensation in the cabins. The **headliner** is the liner under the deck.

LINES, LINE DRAWINGS, PLANS

The arrangement and shape of a boat as shown in scale drawings by a naval architect or yacht designer. Some drawings show the arrangement of rigging and accommodations, others the hull's shape at several sections and from several perspectives, as though slices were taken through the hull.

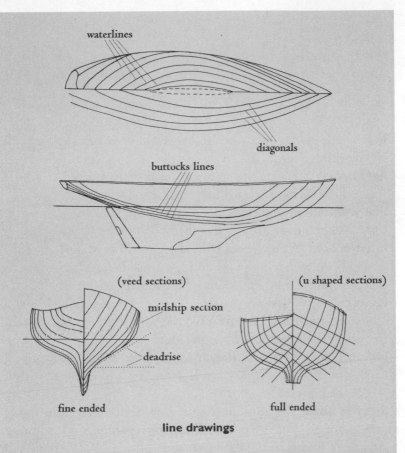

waterlines

diagonals

buttocks lines

(veed sections)

midship section

(u shaped sections)

deadrise

fine ended

full ended

line drawings

- The **sail plan** depicts the sails to be used, the **accommodations plan** the cabin arrangement, the **profile plan** the appearance from the side, the **deck plan** the arrangement on deck, etc.

- The **waterlines plan** shows the hull's shape at several sections, parallel to the water with the boat upright, and reveals how wide the hull is.

- The **buttocks lines** show the hull's shape at several vertical sections and reveal how full the underbody is.

- The midships section shows the shape as though the hull

were cut across amidships, from port to starboard.

A boat with **sweet lines** is handsome and well designed. When a boat **floats on her lines** she is floating as her designer intended her to.

list The lean of a boat when more weight is on one side than on the other.

liveaboard Someone living aboard a boat full time, or a boat ready to be lived aboard full time.

live well An on-deck tank for bait and live fish.

LOA, length over all See length.

lobster boat A powerboat built along the lines of a Maine fishing boat, with a high bow and low topsides aft. If the boat is handsomely finished she may be a **lobster yacht.**

locker A boat's storage (stowage) areas. A **hanging locker** is a closet, a **sail locker** is for sails, a **chain locker** is for ground tackle, a **ski locker** is for water skis.

lock-off, line stopper, halyard stopper, sheet stopper A device that secures and holds a line by squeezing it with a toothed lever.

log, log book 1) A distance-measuring device. The **sum log** is part of a knotmeter. A **taffrail log (patent log)** is towed astern; it also measures speed. 2) A book **(log, log book)** in which the crew records observations concerning the weather, navigation, and other matters. To **log** or **make a log** is to write down this information.

long-ended Having long overhangs. Compare with short-ended.

longitude The angular distance on the earth's surface east or west of the prime meridian at Greenwich, U.K., expressed in degrees and minutes. On a chart or map, **meridians of longitude** run north to south, top to bottom. See prime meridian. Compare with latitude.

longitudinal Running fore and aft.

longshore Alongshore, near shore.

lookout A crewmember watching for danger.

loose-footed Describes a sail whose foot is attached to a boom only at the tack and clew.

loose Slack. A **loose leech** is a floppy leech on a sail. Compare with tight.

LOP See position.

Loran-C An electronic navigation system and instrument. It works by measuring the time difference (T.D.) in reception of radio signals sent by remote transmitters.

lose See let fly.

loudhailer, hailer An electronic voice amplification device.

low Below, away from. A **low-cut jib** has its clew and foot near deck; if the foot touches the deck, the sail is a decksweeper. To steer **low of course** is to steer below course. The **low side** is the leeward side when the boat heels. Compare with high.

lowers See stay.

lubber's line A post in a compass, used as a guide when steering or taking bearings.

luff 1) The forward edge of a sail, except in a parachute spinnaker where it is the windward edge above the spinnaker pole. The **luff curve (luff round, luff hollow)** is a curve that sailmakers build into the luff of a sail to compensate for mast bend or the sag in a stay. 2) A sail that **luffs** is flapping (also light, skinny, soft); compare with fat and full. 3) To **luff (luff up)** is to head up. A **luffing match** occurs when one racing sailboat luffs sharply to prevent another boat from passing to windward.

lull A temporary decrease in wind velocity. See hole.

lunch hook A lightweight anchor. See anchor, hook.

LWL, length on the waterline See length.

"made" A verbal report that a piece of gear is cleated, shackled, or otherwise made fast or secured. See make.

made good, make good A boat's actual speed or course relative to geography, taking into account all factors including the speed and course as shown on the boat's speedometer and compass, the current, waves, and leeway. The speed and course made good are shown on the GPS or Loran-C. The **speed made good** (**SMG,** speed over the bottom, speed over the ground, SOG, **VMG, velocity made good**) is the boat's actual speed. The **course made good** (**CMG,** course over the ground, COG, course over the bottom) is the actual course. Compare with boat speed and course. See track.

magnetic direction A compass direction based on the earth's magnetic field rather than on geography (as with true direction). The direction shown on a magnetic compass. Shown on the compass rose on most charts. Compare with true direction.

main 1) Abbreviation for **mainsail.** 2) Principal or most important. For example, the **main cabin** is the largest cabin, the **mainsail** usually is the largest sail, and the **mainmast** is the tallest mast. In the early days of exploration and empire in the sixteenth century, the South American coast east of Panama was called **the Spanish Main** because it was dominated by Spaniards. 3) A broad expanse. The **bounding main** is all the oceans and seas.

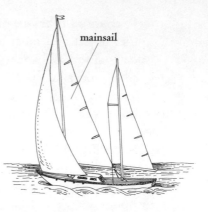

mainsail

mainsail, main Pronounced "main-sul." The sail set behind the mainmast. The **mainsheet** is its sheet.

make 1) See fetch. 2) To **make land** on another boat is to sail faster than her; the land appears to be moving behind her. 3) To **make sail** is to set or hoist the sails. 4) To **make colors** is to raise the ensign. 5) To **make fast** is to connect one object to another securely, for example to shackle a halyard to a sail. See "made."

mal de mer French term for seasickness.

man overboard See crew overboard.

manual Operated by hand rather than electricity or automatically, for example **manual bilge pump**.

Marconi rig See rig.

marina A place in a harbor where many boats are secured to floats and piers.

marine Describes anything specified for use concerning boats or around salt water. For example, **marine fastenings** are screws or bolts made of especially corrosion-resistant materials, and the **marine industry** consists of businesses that build or sell boats and their gear.

mariner Anybody who goes out on the water, usually for commerce but sometimes for pleasure.

marine sanitation device, MSD A toilet and sewage system that satisfies environmental laws. Waste usually goes into a holding tank that is emptied at pump-out stations ashore or on barges.

mark, channel marker, marker, turning mark 1) A buoy or other object that must be passed on a prescribed side so the boat stays in a channel or on a race course. 2) "**Mark**" is a verbal report by the steerer or helmsman that the boat is on course.

marlin tower See tuna tower.

marline Pronounced "marlin." Tarred light line.

marlinespike, fid Pointed spikes several inches long, used to splice line, open jammed knots, etc. A **marlinespike**, often found on a rigging knife, is made of steel, while a **fid** is wooden or steel. **Marlinespike seamanship** comprises the arts of working with and repairing rope, lines, and their fittings.

mast A vertical spar in a sailboat on which sails are set. **Mast bend** is the direction and amount of bend in a mast; see bend. The **mast boot** is a rubber seal around the mast at the partners (at deck level) that prevents water from dripping below. The **mast step** is the support for the mast's bottom (heel). The **masthead** is the top of the mast. The **masthead fly** (apparent wind indicator) is a wind-direction indicator on top of the mast. In a **masthead rig** the jib halyard is at the masthead, unlike the fractional rig; see rig. **Masthead tricolor light,** see navigation lights. **Mast hoops** are wooden rings used to secure the mainsail to the mast in many gaff rigs.

mate In a boat's crew, the captain's chief assistant. The **first mate** is the number-one assistant, the **second mate** is next in authority, and so on. They may be watch captains; see watch.

maxi boat, maxi An offshore racing boat of the maximum allowable size and rating.

mayday Prefix to a radio transmission reporting that the caller is in distress. From the French *m'aidez*—"Help me." Compare with **pan-pan** and **securité**.

mean high water, MHW, mean low water, MLW The average height of high or low tide. The **mean high-water mark** is the line of weed, erosion, or changing color on the shore or a piling at mean high water. See tide.

measurement system A rating rule.

Med moor, Med style A method for docking in which the boat is anchored near a wharf and then tied up to it stern-to. First introduced in harbors in the Mediterranean Sea.

megayacht, superyacht An extremely large, luxurious powerboat or sailboat.

messenger A light line used to haul a heavier line or wire rope through a spar or block.

MHW, mean high water See tide.

midships Amidships.

millibar, mb A unit of atmospheric pressure as shown on a barometer; 1016 mb is equivalent to 30 inches of mercury.

minute $\frac{1}{60}$ of a degree. On most charts 1 minute of latitude (shown at the side) equals 1 nautical mile.

mizzen, jigger The aftermost sail on a ketch or yawl. It is set on the **mizzenmast**. A **mizzen staysail** is a light sail set forward of the mizzenmast.

MLW, mean low water See tide.

MOB See crew overboard.

moderate wind (air, breeze) Wind of 9 to 15 knots.

modified-V See V-bottomed.

mold A recess the shape of the boat, in which fiberglass is laid during construction.

mole A breakwater or other man-made arm constructed of rock that protects a harbor.

MOM, Man Overboard Module A patented device for rescuing somebody from the water using inflatable equipment.

monkey's fist A large knot at the end of a heaving line to provide weight.

monohull A boat with one hull. Compare with multihull.

mooring A permanently set anchor or heavy weight with a strong rode connected to a buoy that is picked up by a boat. A boat on a mooring is **moored**.

motion The boat's pitching, rolling, and heeling. A boat with an **easy motion** is comfortable.

motor Engine, power. A **motorboat** (powerboat) is a boat propelled only by an engine. A **motorsailer** is an auxiliary sailboat with an especially large engine and relatively small sails. A **motoryacht** is a large powerboat.

mouse, mousing To pass light line across the open part of a hook to secure another object. The result is a **mousing**.

mud hole See gunkhole.

multihull A boat with two hulls (catamaran, pontoon boat) or three hulls (trimaran). Compare with monohull.

Mylar A strong synthetic film sometimes laminated to Dacron to make sails.

names of boats See boat names.

narrows A narrow body of water.

National Weather Service, NWS The federal government agency that predicts and reports weather. A division of the National Oceanic and Atmospheric Administration (NOAA), which broadcasts forecasts over its radio system, publishes charts, and provides other services to mariners.

nautical Pertaining to ships, boats, navigation, and sailors. A **nautical mile** is 1.15 statute miles. See knot.

Nautical Almanac An annual publication that includes data necessary or helpful for navigation.

naval architect A designer of ships and boats.

navigable Describes areas of water where boats can be taken without running aground.

navigate, navigation To conduct a boat from one port to another, but more specifically to find the boat's position and determine courses. In **celestial navigation,** the boat's location is found by taking visual sights on the planets with a sextant and then calculating the results using data found in the *Nautical Almanac,* sight reduction tables, and other publications, or in computer software. **Electronic navigation** uses electronic position-finding devices such as GPS. **Coastal navigation** (coastal piloting, coastal pilotage) is navigation near shore using dead reckoning and bearings on buoys and landmarks. Dead reckoning (D.R.) is navigating mainly by tracking the boat's speed and course. (Tradition has it that **dead** here is a mistaken spelling of "ded," or "deduced," but more likely the spelling is correct and the phrase means "exact reckoning.") **Barking dog navigation** is navigating by sound in poor visibility, for example the echo of a dog that is on board or ashore.

navigation aid See aid to navigation.

NAVIGATION LIGHTS, RUNNING LIGHTS

Lights required by the Navigation Rules to be shown at night and in periods of poor visibility to identify a vessel and her course and to warn off other vessels. Each light has a unique purpose. The most important ones are:

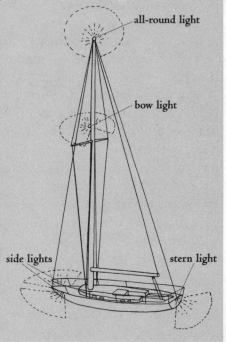

all-round light

bow light

side lights

stern light

- **Running lights,** used only when the boat is under way, include a white **stern light** shining aft, red and green **side lights** shining to port and starboard, and a white **bow light (steaming light)** shining forward to indicate that the boat is under power; smaller boats may show only a 360-degree white **all-round**

light. A **tricolor light** (masthead tricolor) at the top of a sail-boat's mast combines the stern light and side lights.

■ A **riding light** is a white **all-round light** indicating that a boat is anchored at night.

There also are specified lights and light combinations for tug-boats, fishing boats, and other vessels, as well as for many situations. These lights are located on masts, the bow, the stern, and elsewhere.

Navigational Telex, Navtex An electronic system providing weather, navigation, and safety information in a printout.

Navigation Rules, rules of the road The rules prescribing how boats should maneuver near each other, the sound signals they must make, and the lights they must show in order to avoid collision. There are two sets of official rules with a few differences. The **Inland Navigational Rules** govern on U.S. lakes, rivers, and coastal waters. The **International Regulations for Preventing Collisions at Sea (COLREGS, international rules of the road)** govern outer coastal waters and the oceans. See "gross tonnage rule," sound signal and navigation lights, running lights.

navigator, nav The crewmember assigned to keep track of the boat's position, determine courses, and monitor other aspects of navigation. A **navigator's (nav) light** is the light used to view charts. The **navigator's station (nav station)** is the chart table and surrounding area where the navigator does her or his work.

neap tide See tide.

needle and palm See palm and needle.

nicopress To squeeze a metal sleeve (**nicopress sleeve**) onto a wire in order to make a loop. Compare with swage.

NOAA See National Weather Service.

no-go zone The wind's eye and several degrees to either side of it. If a sailboat is steered here, her sails luff and she makes no headway.

nonskid, nonslip, anti-skid Describes a surface treated so it provides good traction.

NOOD, National Offshore One-Design regatta A regatta held for racing sailboats.

nor'easter, northeaster A storm in which the wind blows hard from the northeast. Most nor'easters are wet, meaning that there is rain, but there are some dry nor'easters.

Notice to Mariners A periodic government publication that describes hazards, changes in buoys, and other news of interest to mariners.

no-wake zone See wake.

numbers, numbering Registration numbers required by state laws to be displayed on the bow.

nun, nun buoy See buoy, buoyage.

nylon Stretchy, strong fiber used usually in spinnakers and anchor rodes.

oar See rowboat.

obstruction An object in or near the water requiring a boat to make a major course alteration to pass to one side.

ocean race, offshore race, long-distance race, distance race A sailboat or powerboat race on the ocean or a large lake and/or lasting longer than a day. The sport is called **ocean (offshore) racing,** and the participants are **ocean (offshore) racers.** Compare with around the buoys.

off Away from. To steer **off course** is to steer the wrong course. **Off the bow** is to one side or another of directly ahead. To sail **off the wind** is to sail on a run, with the wind astern. To **head off** is to change course downwind. Compare with on.

off the wind

offshore Away from shore and toward deep water. An **offshore boat** is designed for ocean use. An **offshore wind** blows from the land over water.

oilcan See pant.

oilskins, oilers Foul-weather gear.

Old Man An affectionate nickname for the captain or skipper.

on Directly. To steer **on course** is to steer on the correct course. An object **on the bow** is ahead or slightly to one side, **on the beam** (abeam) is alongside, **on the quarter** is between on the beam and astern, and **on the stern** is astern or slightly to one side. To sail **on the wind** is to sail close-hauled, with sails trimmed tight. Compare with off.

on the wind

on board, aboard In or on a boat.

one-design A boat built to the same design as other boats.

one-off See custom boat.

on the run Letting go a line quickly and completely.

open boat A boat with very little (if any) deck.

open water Out in an ocean, broad lake, or other large body of water where there is no land to provide protection from wind and waves. Compare with shelter.

operator's license A state license to operate a pleasure boat. Compare with certificate.

outboard Outside a boat's rail. An **outboard engine (outboard)** is hung on the rail or transom, and is mounted on an **outboard bracket**. Compare with inboard.

outdrive See inboard/outboard drive.

outfit To equip a boat.

outhaul The line that adjusts the position of the clew and the tension of the foot of a sail on a boom.

outrigger A spar projecting from a vessel's side to support a small boat, a sail, fishing gear, or a flopper-stopper.

overboard In the water outside the boat. See crew overboard.

overcanvassed With too much sail set.

overhang The distance that the bow and stern extend beyond the waterline. The **forward overhang** is at the bow, the **after overhang** at the stern.

overhaul 1) To overtake another boat. 2) To inspect or prepare gear.

overlapped, overlapping A sail or boat partially alongside another. The **overlap** is the distance that they are alongside.

overnight To go on a brief one- or two-day cruise. An **overnighter** is a boat with a cuddy or small cabin and skimpy accommodations. Compare with cruise and weekend.

overpowered, overcanvassed Out of control due to too much engine power, or sails that are too large.

override A tangle between turns of a line on a winch.

overrigged With a mast and other rigging that are too large or heavy. Compare with underrigged.

overstand To fetch a buoy or destination with room to spare.

overtake To catch from astern.

over the bottom, over the ground See made good.

overtrim To trim too far.

owner's flag See private signal.

![P](letter P)

package boat A new boat that comes from the manufacturer prepared for use so there is no need to purchase optional equipment.

packing gland See stuffing box.

padeye A metal eye on a small plate. Blocks, lines, and other objects are shackled to the eye.

padeye

paid hand A crewmember who is paid money.

painter A towing or docking line at the bow of a dinghy.

palm and needle A leather glove and needles used with thread for sewing.

panel 1) A clearly defined section of a mast, sail, liner, or other object. 2) The control center for electrical and other switches.

pan-pan Rhymes with "con-con." An alert used at the beginning of a radiotelephone transmission to report an urgent safety-related message concerning another boat. Compare with mayday and securité.

pant, oilcan For a boat's side or bottom to flex.

parachute A type of spinnaker or flare.

parallel rulers A navigation tool consisting of two wooden or plastic strips linked and held parallel by arms. It is used to transfer bearings and courses to and from the compass rose on a chart.

paravane See flopper-stopper.

parbuckle A device for hoisting an object onto the deck. A line or strap is secured on deck, then passed over the side and under the object, and then hauled from deck or by a halyard. As the line or strap is tensioned, the object rolls up the topsides.

part 1) To break. 2) See tackle.

partners The deck opening through which the mast passes.

parts of the boat The hull, rigging, sails, spars, and their components.

passage 1) A navigable channel between two bodies of water. 2) A nonstop trip in a boat, longer than a day from one point to the next. **Passages** are legs of a voyage. **Passagemaking** is long-distance cruising, **coastal passagemaking** is near shore, **ocean passagemaking** is offshore, on either the ocean or a large lake.

passageway A corridor between cabins.

patent log See log.

pawl A hinged pin in a winch that keeps the winch from backing off, or turning in the wrong direction.

pay off See head off.

pay out To ease an anchor rode, docking line, or other long line that is under strain a long distance. Compare with let go and let fly, lose.

peak In the gaff rig, the after end of the gaff. It is raised and lowered using a **peak halyard.**

pedestal A support for a steering wheel, winch, windlass, or other gear. **Pedestal steering** is a steering system with a wheel on a pedestal.

pelican hook A long hook that looks somewhat like a pelican's bill.

pendant Pronounced "pennant." A short length of wire, chain, or line used for a specialized purpose. A **mooring pendant** secures the boat to the mooring, a **tack pendant** raises the sail above waves.

pennant A flag. Compare with pendant.

performance, high-performance 1) Speed. **High performance** may indicate exceptionally high speed. 2) Fast. A **performance (high-performance) boat** is faster than other boats of her type.

Performance Handicap Racing Fleet, PHRF A handicap system used in sailboat racing. Handicaps are assigned by a committee based on observed performance.

period The distance between waves.

permanent backstay See stay.

personal gear Equipment used or carried by an individual, for example a personal flotation device (PFD). Compare with ship's gear, which may include a life raft for the entire crew.

personal watercraft, PWC A small one- or two-person jet-driven boat ridden on a saddle. One brand is the Jet Ski.

PFD, personal flotation device, personal buoyancy A life-saving buoyant device worn or held by a person, including life jackets, life vests (which are less bulky than life jackets), float coats, cushions, horseshoes, and life rings. The Coast Guard categorizes them (Type I through Type V) by shape and buoyancy. Buoyancy in most PFDs is provided by foam. In an **inflatable PFD** buoyancy is air provided by the wearer or a CO_2 cartridge. See buoyancy and inflatable.

phase characteristics See light.

phonetic alphabet Names assigned to letters in order to prevent confusion among ones with similar sounds during radio transmissions and other communications. For example "Mike" stands for "M" and "November" for "N."

pier A narrow platform providing access from the shore to deeper water. It either floats or is fixed on pilings built out into the water. A **finger pier** is a narrow floating pier leading off from a pier or wharf.

pig stick A flagstaff on which the burgee or private signal is set. The pig stick is hoisted aloft on the flag halyard and holds the flag above the sails.

piling, pile A post driven into the water's bottom and supporting a pier, wharf, jetty, dock, or float.

pilot 1) To navigate near shore. **Piloting, pilotage,** coastal navigation, see navigate. 2) A professional seaman who navigates vessels into ports and harbors. A **pilot boat** takes pilots from shore out to boats waiting to enter harbor. A number of items have been inspired by pilots. A **pilothouse** is a cabin at or near deck level containing a steering wheel and instruments. A **pilot berth** is a narrow bunk under the side deck. A **pilot cracker** is a large, thick, pasty cracker. **Automatic pilot, autopilot,** see self-steerer.

pilot books Government publications providing information about navigation, harbors, etc.

pilot charts Publications showing probable weather conditions and current patterns in the oceans and seas.

pin 1) A turning mark in a race course. 2) A clevis, cotter, or shear pin.

pinch, squeeze, feather To sail so close to the wind that the sails are slightly luffing. See high.

pintle A fitting for attaching an outboard rudder to a transom. It is a rod that fits into an eye (gudgeon).

pitch 1) The rise and fall of the bow and stern. Compare with pound. 2) **Propeller pitch,** see propeller.

pitchpole When a boat somersaults stern over bow.

plane, planing boat "Plane" rhymes with "main." For a boat to skim across the water rather than plow through it. **Planing boats (hulls)** are lightweight and have relatively large engines or sails. **Nonplaning (displacement) boats** are relatively heavy ones that cannot lift out, and their speed generally is limited to their hull speed.

plans See lines.

play 1) Shaking due to a loose fit. **Play in the helm** may be due to a loose steering cable. 2) To **play a sheet (play a sail)** is to pay constant attention to sail trim.

plot To keep track of a boat's position, track, and bearings on a chart, either manually or electronically. **The plot** (for example **the D.R. plot**) is the record of bearings and positions on a chart. A **plotter** (electronic or manual) is a device that assists in making a plot.

plug 1) A wooden object shoved into a hole. 2) A form used to make the molds that are required in fiberglass construction.

plumb Straight, vertical. On a **plumb bow** the stem is vertical.

ply Plywood. **Marine ply** is especially resistant to water.

pneumatic Inflatable or driven by air power.

point 1) In sailing, to steer close to the wind. **Pointing ability** is the boat's ability to sail close to the wind. 2) A **point of land** is land projecting into the water.

point ship To turn a vessel end for end at anchor or mooring using lines.

points of sail Sailing directions relative to the wind. The three

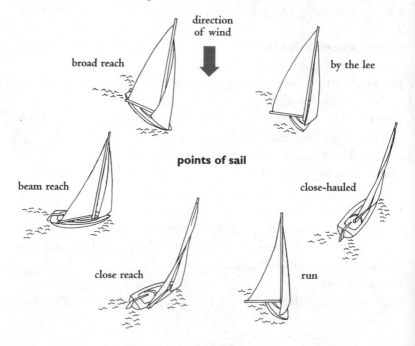

direction
of wind

broad reach

by the lee

points of sail

beam reach

close-hauled

close reach

run

points of sail are running, reaching, and sailing close-hauled.

pole out See wing-and-wing.

polyester Synthetic white sailmaking fiber used to make mainsails and jibs. One trade name is Dacron.

polypropylene A synthetic material used to make buoyant rope and clothing.

pontoon An inflated hull of a catamaran-type powerboat, for example a houseboat.

pooped Filled with water by a large wave from astern.

poptop A cabintop that can be raised to provide standing headroom below.

port 1) The left-hand side of a boat when the crew is facing the bow. When a sailboat is on the **port tack,** the wind is coming over the **port side.** Compare with starboard. 2) A commercial harbor. 3) See porthole.

port captain A harbormaster.

porthole, port A small window in a boat.

position A boat's location as plotted on a chart in terms of **geographic position** (longitude and latitude) or relative to landmarks and aids to navigation. **Position finding** is the science (and often the art) of finding where you are on the water. A **dead-reckoning position (D.R.)** is based on a record of the boat's speed and course. An **estimated position (E.P.)** is the best estimate of a boat's position based on dead reckoning and one bearing. A **line of position (LOP)** is a compass bearing or other charted line on which a boat is located. A **circle of position (COP)** is part of an arc of equal distance from a charted object. See distance off. When two or more reliable lines of position are crossed, the boat has a **fixed position** (fix). See navigate and plot.

pound When the bow violently smashes down on the water.

power, powered 1) Concerning the engine. To be **under power** is to have the engine on and in gear. The **power plant** is the engine, the **power train** the transmission, or linkage between the engine and propeller. To **power** (motor) or be **under**

power is to make way under the force of the engine. 2) Force. To **power up** is to make the sails more full. **Driving power** is a boat's ability to sail with stability in strong winds. **Holding power** is an anchor's ability to be secure in the bottom.

powerboat, motorboat, power vessel A boat propelled only by an engine. Compare with auxiliary. A **powerboater** is someone who uses power-boats for pleasure.

power cruiser A powerboat with accommodations. See cruiser, express cruiser, sedan cruiser, trawler.

power cruiser

powerful Large and capable of going fast or handling rough weather. A large, full bow is a **powerful bow.**

powerhead The cover of the cylinders in an outboard motor.

Power Squadrons, USPS The United States Power Squadrons, a national boating organization with many local and regional chapters.

pram A flat-bottomed blunt-bowed dinghy.

pratique See quarantine.

prefeeder See feeder.

pressure A term for wind used by some racing sailors, usually in the context of a puff or gust. **Pressure ahead** means that the wind is increasing ahead.

pressure water, pressure system An onboard water system run by an electric pump.

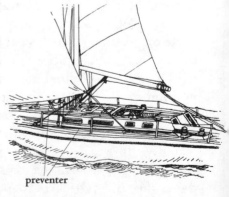

prestretched rope Rope that has been specially treated to minimize stretch.

prevailing wind The wind

preventer

that usually blows in a particular location.

preventer A line or device that stops a boom from swinging across the boat.

primaries, primary winches The largest sheet winches, which are used for the primary and most demanding task of trimming the largest jibs and spinnakers.

prime meridian, Greenwich meridian, Greenwich Mean Time, GMT, Zulu The prime (Greenwich) meridian is at zero degrees longitude, at Greenwich, U.K. The time along the meridian is **Greenwich Mean Time (GMT, Zulu)** and is the standard time for navigation and other purposes around the world.

prismatic coefficient Used by naval architects and yacht designers, it is a measure of a hull's fineness. It compares the boat's actual displaced volume with the volume of a theoretical shape the length of the boat's waterline and the width of the boat's maximum beam at the waterline. A boat with a high number is full-ended, one with a low number is fine-ended.

private signal, owner's flag A flag custom-designed with a unique symbol for a boat's owner. When flown it indicates that the person is on board.

privileged vessel Outdated term for stand-on vessel.

production boat A stock boat.

profile plan A part of the lines.

PROPELLER, PROP, SCREW, WHEEL

The bladed device that propels a boat through the water under power. A **single propeller (prop, screw)** is one propeller, **twin (dual) propellers** are two. A **slow-turning propeller** is large and makes relatively few revolutions per minute, a **fast-turning propeller** is small and revolves more frequently.

The blades on a **folding propeller** fold up into a tubular shape when the engine is off, in order to reduce water resistance.

For the same reason, the blades on a **feathering propeller** turn their edges toward the water flow when the engine is off.

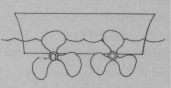
twin propellers

Propeller pitch is the angle of the blade, or, more technically, the distance the propeller would travel in one rotation if there were no **propeller slip,** the inevitable slight loss of efficiency. With a **variable-pitch propeller,** the pitch is adjusted when the boat is under way, for optimum efficiency.

Propeller torque is the sideways push of a propeller. A **right-handed propeller** turns clockwise when viewed from astern. When the engine is in forward gear, a right-handed propeller pushes the stern to starboard and the bow to port. A **left-handed propeller** turns counterclockwise and pushes the bow to starboard. **Counterrotating propellers** are twin propellers that turn in opposite directions to eliminate walk, the boat's tendency to be pushed to one side by her propellers.

A **propeller aperture** is a notch in the keel or rudder for a propeller under water. A **surfacing drive (surface-piercing drive) propeller** is mostly above the water rather than below it; its blades barely touch the water.

proper Correct or suitable. A **proper yacht** is a boat that is just right in design, construction, appearance, and finish. A **proper line** (or other piece of gear) is suitably strong for the job at hand. **Proper course,** see course.

protected Describes a harbor or other body of water that has land or a breakwater between it and deep water to block large waves.

protest An allegation of a foul or infraction of the racing rules. A ruling is made after a **protest hearing** by the regatta's jury or **protest committee.**

provisions Food, water, and other necessities. To **provision a boat** is to bring provisions aboard.

prow Antiquated term for bow.

puff, puffer A quick, moderate, and short increase in wind speed. Compare with gust.

pulling boat A rowboat.

pulpit, guardrails, liferails A steel rail around the bow or the stern. The **stern pulpit** is sometimes called a "pushpit."

pump 1) A device for moving liquids, for example the **bilge pump**. Also to work a pump. 2) To trim and ease a sail rapidly to speed up a racing sailboat.

pump-out station Where sewage is pumped out of a holding tank. See marine sanitation device.

purchase See tackle.

push See drive.

pushpit Stern pulpit.

PWC Personal watercraft.

pyrotechnic A flare.

quadrant 1) A curved metal structure used in some steering systems to connect the steering wheel. 2) **Dangerous quadrant,** see dangerous semicircle.

quarantine Restrictions on a newly arrived crew's activities in a port until they have received clearance *(pratique)* from local health officials.

quarter, quartering A side of the boat near the stern. A **quarter berth** is a bed under a side deck and far aft. A **quartering sea (quartering wind)** is from abaft the beam but not directly astern. A buoy or other object off the boat that is lying between abeam and astern and on the starboard (port) side is described as being **on the starboard (port) quarter.**

quick stop A tactic for effecting crew overboard rescue. Immediately after the victim falls over, the boat turns tight circles around him or her in order to maintain visibility and to facilitate making contact with a line or recovery device.

race 1) Competition. The **race course** is the route required to complete the race. A **match race** is between two boats (for example in the America's Cup), a **team race** is between two teams of three or four boats, a **fleet race** is among several boats. A **race committee** is a group of officials who run a sailboat race. 2) **Tide (tidal) race,** see tide.

racer-cruiser, cruiser-racer, dual-purpose boat A sailboat that is fast and has comfortable accommodations.

racing machine, racer, stripped-out racer A sailboat or powerboat with very few comfort features that is designed and used primarily for racing.

racing rules The Racing Rules of Sailing, written and imposed by the International Sailing Federation. They govern the conduct of racing sailboats. Beginning in 1997 these rules comprise the **simplified racing rules,** which are less complex than the old rules. Infractions of the racing rules are fouls. The rules are enforced by the race participants and by officials serving as the regatta's judges or members of the jury or protest committee. See protest.

racon A device that sends a signal when it senses a vessel's radar. Often installed on buoys and other aids to navigation to make them more visible.

radar An electronic device that detects objects at a distance and shows their location and bearing on a monitor (**radar scope**). **Radar arch,** see arch. A **radar reflector** is hoisted in the rigging to make a vessel visible on another vessel's radar. See racon.

radial cut, radial clew, radial head Describe a sail whose seams extend fingerlike from the corners toward the middle to control stretch. Compare with crosscut.

radio direction finder, RDF An electronic navigation device that takes bearings on radio signals.

radiotelephone A radio transmitter and receiver linking a boat with other boats and the shore. The common types are very high frequency radio (VHF-FM), whose range usually is less than about 60 miles, and single-sideband radio (SSB), which has a much greater range.

raft up To tie boats side by side when one or more of them are at anchor.

rage Bahamian term for heavy weather. When there is a **rage at the bar,** waves break wildly at the mouth of a harbor.

rail The outer edge of the deck where it meets the gunwale (pronounced "gunnel") at the top of the topside. The rail sometimes is raised to stop waves and provide a toerail.

raise 1) To hoist. 2) To sight an object.

raised bridge Fly bridge.

raised deck A flush deck.

rake The angle of the mast, bow, or transom. If vertical it has no rake. Otherwise it is **raked aft** or **raked forward.**

ramp Launching ramp. See launch.

range 1) In navigation, a pair of objects that when lined up one behind the other indicate the channel. 2) Distance to an object. The **range and bearing** to a waypoint or other point is its distance and the course to it. A **rangefinder** is an instrument used to determine distance to an object. See stability, tide, visibility.

rating rule, rating system A method for handicapping a sailboat race so boats of different sizes and designs may compete. A boat's potential speed is predicted by entering her measurements into a formula to produce a number (the rating). The rating is then applied to the length and type of course to produce time allowances. One rating rule is the International Measurement System (IMS). See first. Compare with handicap.

RDF Radio direction finder.

reach 1) The point of sail on which a boat sails across the wind. On a **beam reach** the wind is dead abeam, 90 degrees from the course. On a **close reach** the wind is between about 60 and 90 degrees (also called sailing shy). On a **broad reach** the wind is on the quarter, between 90 and about 170 degrees. A **reacher** is special spinnaker or jib used when reaching. A **reaching strut** is a short spar that holds the spinnaker afterguy away from the shrouds on a beam or close reach. "Jockey pole" in Britain. 2) A narrow body of water between an island and the mainland.

"ready about" A verbal warning to prepare for a tack when sailing. It is followed by "hard alee" ("lee-oh"). Compare with "stand by."

reciprocal course The course opposite to the current course, or 180 degrees in the other direction. See Williamson turn.

red sector See sector.

reef 1) A barely submerged line of rocks or land. 2) To make a sail smaller. In **roller reefing,** the sail is either rolled

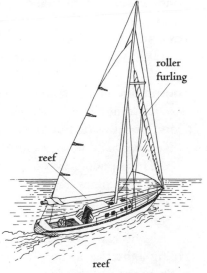

roller furling

reef

reef

around a wire at its luff or lowered a few feet and rolled

around the boom. In **jiffy, slab,** or **tied-in reefing,** the sail is lowered a few feet, a strain is taken on the bottom of the sail with **reefing lines** (earings) passed through **reef cringles** in the sail, and the halyard is tightened. The excess sail material may be secured to the foot with light lines **(reef points).** A **flattening reef** is a very small reef taken to flatten the bottom part of the sail. To **shake out a reef** is to take it out. A **reef knot** is a square knot.

reeve, rove To lead or pass a line through a block or eye. A line that has been led is **rove.**

reflector Something that makes an object more visible by reflecting radar signals or light. **Reflective tape,** which reflects light, is placed on buoys, PFDs, foul-weather gear, and other objects. A **radar reflector** reflects radar signals. Compare with racon.

regatta A scheduled race or series of races.

relief, relieve Replacement, replace. **Relieving tackle,** see tackle.

render A line's movement as it is eased through a block.

rendezvous A gathering of boats away from their hailing ports.

resin See fiberglass.

reverse Opposite to the usual. A **reverse transom** slopes forward toward the deck. **Reverse sheer** is humped rather than hollow.

rhumb line The straight course between two points. See great circle route.

ride A boat's situation in the water. To **ride at anchor** is to be anchored and move around as the wind shifts. In a **hard ride** the boat pounds and slaps the water uncomfortably, in a **soft ride** she comes down easily. There is considerable spray in a **wet ride,** but none in a **dry ride.** To **ride easy (easily)** is to move comfortably. To **ride out a storm** is to survive a storm, gale, or heavy weather by using a storm tactic. See storm.

riding light See anchor, hook.

riding sails See steadying sails.

RIG

To **rig** is to prepare the boat or her components for use. To **unrig** is to take the boat or its components apart. To **jury rig** is to make a quick, expedient repair in an emergency.

The rig consists of the spars, fishing gear, trailer, etc. and their attached equipment. The usual sailboat rigs are

- The old **square rig** (set by **square-riggers**) had most sails set athwartships on yards.

- Most sailboats today use the **fore-and-aft rig**, with most sails set lengthwise on booms. There are variations on the fore-and-aft rig:

  The **Marconi (Bermudian, jib-headed) rig** is the modern sailing fore-and-aft rig, with a three-sided mainsail defined by the mast and boom. (Reportedly first used in Bermuda, it seemed so tall when it first appeared on large boats in the 1920s that people compared it to the towering radio transmitters built by Guglielmo Marconi.)

gaff-rigged cat boat

  The **gaff rig** is low and has four sides defined by the mast, boom, and gaff. The mainsail's luff is attached to the mast using mast hoops, wooden rings around the mast that slide up and down as the throat halyard is raised and lowered.

sloop

  The **lateen rig**, used on the popular Sunfish class of sailboats, has a boom projecting forward of the stubby mast where it connects with a sprit that extends aloft at a sharp angle to support the sail's head.

- There are three single-masted rigs: the **sloop rig,** with the mast less than one-third of the overall length abaft the headstay; the cutter, whose mast is more than one-third of the boat's overall length abaft the headstay; and the **cat rig,** which does not have a jib.

cutter

- The **multimasted rig (divided rig, split rig)** has two or more masts in three combinations:

ketch

    The **yawl,** a two-masted sailboat whose after mast (the mizzenmast) is smaller than the forward mast (mainmast) and located abaft the rudder post.

    The **ketch,** a two-masted sailboat whose mizzenmast is smaller than the mainmast and located forward of the rudder post.

gaff-rigged schooner

    The **cat ketch** or **cat yawl** carries two cat-rigged masts, with no jib.

    The **schooner,** in which the most forward mast (the foremast) is shorter than the after masts.

- Sailboat rigs are also known by where the headstay attaches to the mast and by how many stays it has forward of the mainmast:

    The **masthead rig**—the jib halyard is at the masthead.

    The **fractional rig**—the headstay intersects the mast partway down from the masthead.

The **double-headsail (double-head, cutter) rig** has two
stays, the headstay and the forestay (running aloft inside
the headstay). Of the two jibs, the one on the headstay is
the jib, the one on the forestay the forestaysail (staysail).

See overrigged, stay, tall ship, underrigged, wishbone boom.

rigging The masts, booms, tuna towers, and the wires that support the rig are the **standing rigging**. The ropes, blocks, and
other movable gear that adjust sails and equipment set on the
standing rigging make up the **running rigging**.

rigging knife A knife with a long blade, a marlinespike, and
(often) a slot used to unscrew the clevis pins that are in screw
shackles.

rigging screw British term for turnbuckle.

rigging terminal Fitting that connects the end of a stay or
other wire to a turnbuckle or other fitting. See swage.

right To bring a boat upright after a capsize. A **self-righting
boat** can be righted without outside assistance. The **righting
arm** is the force that provides a boat's stability and resists capsize. It is characterized as an arm (as in "lever arm") because
it works like a lever whose fulcrum is the center of buoyancy
(the locus of all flotation). The end of this "lever" is the
boat's center of gravity (the locus of all weights holding her
down). The farther the center of gravity is from the center of
buoyancy in the direction away from the boat's rail, the longer
is the arm and the more stable is the boat.

right of way The right granted to a vessel by the Navigation
Rules (rules of the road) to continue on the present course
without giving way to another vessel. That vessel is the **right-
of-way vessel,** (also stand-on vessel).

riprap Piles of stone that protect a breakwater, jetty, lighthouse,
or pier from erosion.

roach The convex or concave curve in a sail's leech or foot when
seen from the side.

road, roads, roadstead A partly protected anchorage.

rocker The curve of the bottom of the hull from bow to stern when seen from the side. The deeper the curve, the greater the rocker.

rocket launcher A tube recessed in a powerboat's rail to hold a vertical fishing rod.

rode Anchor rode.

rod rigging Stays made of steel rod, which stretches less than wire rope.

Rod-stop A tactic for slowing and steadying a sailboat, devised by Roderick Stephens, Jr. The jib is doused, the mainsail is pushed out all the way to the leeward shrouds, and the boat is steered on a close reach about 60 degrees off the wind.

rogue wave See wave.

roll To put one rail down, then the other. In a **roll tack (roll jibe)** a racing sailboat is rolled by her crew in order to increase the apparent wind speed aloft and speed up the boat.

roller furler A device that douses a sail by rolling it up around itself, usually on a wire, so the crew need not lower it. A roller furler may also be used to reef a sail by **roller reefing**.

room to maneuver See sea room.

rooster tail A small, steep ridge of water in the wake of a fast-moving boat.

rope A length of cordage. When cut up for use on a boat it becomes "line." The only rope on a boat is the **boltrope**. Most rope is **braided**, or woven in a complex weave; **double-braided rope** has a core inside a sleeve. In **laid rope (stranded rope)**, three or four large strands are twisted around each other; its lay is the direction in which the strands twist (to right or left).

round-bottomed Describes a boat whose bottom is curved. Compare with flat-bottomed, V-bottomed.

round off, round up Head off or up sharply.

rove See reeve.

rowboat, pulling boat A boat propelled manually by a **rower**

(oarsman) using an oar, a long rod with a paddle or blade at one end. When the oarsman pulls the other end, the oar pivots at the boat's rail in a **rowlock** (oarlock), and the blade pulls through the water, providing propulsion.

rubbing strake, rubwale A strip of rubber or wood on a boat's side protecting her rail from objects alongside. Compare with fender.

RUDDER

The underwater fin usually located near or at the stern and controlled by the helm to steer the boat. The **rudder blade** is the wing-shaped portion under water. **Dual (twin) rudders** are two rudders used on sailing multihulls or especially beamy monohulls. There is one on each side so that one rudder is completely in the water when the boat heels.

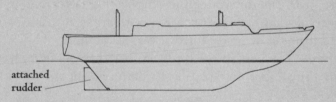

attached rudder

The **rudder post** is the shaft in the hull that connects the helm (tiller or wheel) to the rudder through the **rudder stock,** a rod in the forward part of the rudder.

- An **outboard rudder (transom-mounted rudder)** hangs off the stern on gudgeons and pintles. A **canting rudder** swings sideways as the boat heels so it remains vertical and provides best performance. A **popup rudder** lifts in shallow water.

- An **inboard rudder** is under the hull; it is suspended from and pivots on the **rudder stock,** which connects to the **rudder post,** which is turned by the helm.

• Among different types of inboard rudders, an **attached rudder** is hung on the aft edge of the keel, while a **separate rudder** is remote from the keel. A separate rudder may be hung on a skeg (a small fin) or it may be a **spade rudder,** not supported by either a skeg or the keel. If a spade rudder projects forward of the stock it is a **balanced rudder.**

rudder-action signal See sound signal.

rules of the road See Navigation Rules.

run 1) The point of sail on which the wind is astern. **To run before it (run off, run with it,** scud) is a storm tactic that involves sailing slowly on a run in heavy weather. 2) To lead or direct. To **run the jibsheet forward** is to pull the end of the sheet forward. 3) The boat's bottom under the stern. A **flat run** is a flat bottom. 4) A boating trip lasting a day or less. 5) To **run out your time,** a navigation tactic used in fog, is to calculate how long it will take to arrive at a destination, and then sail or power for that period of time.

runabout The basic powerboat. Smaller than about 25 feet, it has a small deck and, usually, an outboard engine.

running attitude The vertical angle a powerboat hull makes to the water when under way.

running backstay, runner See stay.

running gear The propellers, rudders, and other equipment needed for a powerboat to operate.

running lights See navigation lights.

running rigging See rigging.

S

safe leeward position See leeward.

safety at sea The branch of seamanship especially concerned with saving lives and dealing with emergencies.

safety harness A harness worn by a boater and attached to the boat or a jackline with a webbed tether to keep the boater on board.

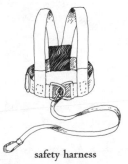

safety harness

Safety of Life at Sea Conference, SOLAS An international organization, a part of the International Maritime Organization, that establishes standards for maritime safety.

sag Move or slide to leeward. When a boat **sags off to leeward** she slides. The headstay **sags** when the jib is full.

SAIL

As a verb, a sailboat **sails,** her crew **goes sailing.** When a boat **sails around her anchor (mooring),** she swings around the anchor rode or mooring with the wind, sometimes violently, even though her sails are not set. Her mast and hull catch the wind.

As a noun, a sailboat's means of propulsion. Pronounced as

spelled when used alone, pronounced "sul" when attached to other words, like **mainsail, staysail, topsail.** The **sail plan** is the design of the rig and sails in a profile view. The **sail area (S.A.)** is the area of the sails in square feet or square meters; a **500-square-foot sail** has an area of 500 square feet. **Sailcloth** is the fabric used to make sails. A **sailmaker** is a professional manufacturer of sails working in a **sail loft.**

Sail handling is the art of managing sails. To **set a sail (set sail)** or hoist a sail is to pull it up. To **trim a sail** is to adjust the sail's shape. To **douse a sail** is to lower it or roll it up on a roller furler. To **furl a sail** is to fold and secure it on a boom using a **sail stop (sail tie,** gasket).

The **sail inventory (suit of sails)** consists of all the sails on board. They include **working sails,** the mainsail and a jib used in normal conditions, plus some or all of the following:

- **Light sails** are the spinnaker and other lightweight sails set on a run or reach.

- **Riding sails** are small sails set on sail- and powerboats to limit rolling.

- **Storm sails,** set in heavy weather, are a very small **mainsail** and jib (**storm trysail** and storm jib).

- A **topsail** is a sail set above another sail.

- A **staysail** is a small sail set inside or below another sail. See staysail.

Sail controls are lines used to trim the sail and adjust its shape, including the halyard, sheet, traveler, Cunningham, and downhaul. **Sail shape** is the draft and appearance as created by the sailmaker and adjusted by the **sail trimmers** in the crew. A **sail slide** or **sail hank (sail slug)** is a metal or plastic device that secures a sail to a mast or stay. When sails are not in use they are stowed in **sail bags** or under **sail covers.**

See jib and spinnaker.

sail-area/displacement ratio, S.A./D ratio A number that indicates how much driving force a sailboat has relative to her weight. The higher the number, the greater the driving force.

sailboard, board, Windsurfer A sailboat about 12 feet long and sailed by a standing person who holds up the mast and sail. One type is the **Windsurfer**. To sail a sailboard is to go **boardsailing** or **windsurfing**. A sailor on a sailboard is a **boardsailor**.

sailer/sailor A word ending "er" refers to a boat, for example **motorsailer**, while **sailor** (ending "or") refers to a person who uses a sailboat.

saloon On larger boats the cabin used for entertaining and eating. Sometimes "salon."

salvage To save a boat after she has been abandoned by her crew. The term also refers to the objects saved.

samson post See bitt.

sand yacht A sailboat that rides on wheels over land.

sandwich construction See fiberglass.

Santa Ana A strong easterly wind that blows offshore from Southern California's desert.

SAR See search-and-rescue mission

satellite navigation, satnav See Global Positioning System (GPS).

sausage A long, tubular sail bag in which the sail is rolled up or flaked.

scale See chart.

scantlings The materials and other specifications for a vessel's construction.

schooner See rig.

scoop, air scoop The cowl in a ventilator.

scope 1) The angle of the anchor rode to the water's bottom as indicated by the ratio between,

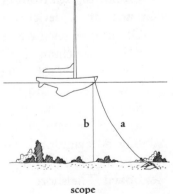

scope

on one hand, a) the length of rode paid out and, on the other hand, b) the water's depth plus the freeboard. For example when the crew on a boat whose freeboard is 5 feet pays out 105 feet of rode while anchoring in a depth of 20 feet, there is 5:1 **scope.** To **let out scope** is to let out more rode, thereby **increasing scope.** 2) **Radar scope,** see radar.

scow 1) A fast, flat-bottomed, blunt-bowed racing sailboat popular on small lakes. Most have leeboards. 2) Around salt water, a derogatory term for a slow, bulky boat like a **garbage scow.**

screw Propeller.

scud 1) To run before the wind in heavy weather. See run. 2) The broken clouds often seen during a storm. **Scuddy weather** is stormy.

scull To propel a boat with a single oar worked over the stern or by swinging the rudder back and forth.

scupper A drain in the deck, gunwale, or cockpit.

scuttle To deliberately sink a vessel by driving or opening holes in her bottom.

sea 1) Deep water well away from land. To be offshore is to be **at sea** or **on the high seas. Sea stories** are tales told about boats and the sea. 2) The **sea (sea condition)** is the general condition of the surrounding water, while **seas** are individual waves and swells. In a **head sea** the waves are from ahead, in a **following sea** from behind.

sea anchor A device used to limit drifting far from shore. Often used when riding out storms, it is a parachute deployed off the bow at the end of a line to keep the bow pointed into the waves. Sometimes "storm anchor." See storm. Compare with drogue.

sea anchor

seabag A cylindrical fabric bag for carrying clothes and gear.

seaboard The shore.

seaboots Waterproof boots with nonskid soles.

sea breeze, lake breeze, onshore wind Wind blowing from the water toward the shore.

sea bucket A bucket, traditionally made of canvas, used to scoop water while the boat is moving.

seacock A bronze or plastic valve that closes and opens a through-hull to allow water to enter or exhaust. **Ball-valve seacocks** shut and open using movable balls, **gate-valve seacocks** use sliding gates.

sea condition The relative roughness of the water.

seafarer A person at home in a boat at sea.

seagoing Describes a boat or person capable of going to sea.

seakindly Describes a boat comfortable in heavy weather. See forgiving.

seaman, seawoman An especially knowledgeable sailor.

seamanship The art and science of handling a boat competently and safely in all conditions. A task performed capably is done in a **seamanlike manner**.

search-and-rescue mission, SAR An official search for a distressed vessel.

sea room, room to maneuver, room The space needed by a boat to avoid a collision or another danger.

seas Waves. **Short seas**, see chop.

seasickness, *mal de mer* Motion sickness in a boat.

sea trials A test run in a boat.

Seattle sling See Lifesling.

seawall A wharf or other waterfront area supported by bulkheads or braces.

seaway An area of relatively steep waves from different directions.

seaworthy Able to survive rough weather. Describes a boat with a sturdy hull, strong rig, and excellent stability.

section A drawing showing the shape of a boat as though she were sliced open.

sector The arc in which a lighthouse's light is visible. A **danger**

(red) sector is a portion of the light showing red to warn navigators away from shoals or land.

secure To hold in place, make fast, tie down. Something that is secured will not budge.

securité Pronounced "saycuritay." A French word said over a radiotelephone to warn other boats of danger. Compare with mayday and pan-pan.

sedan cruiser, convertible cruiser A power cruiser 25 feet or longer with a fly bridge and accommodations in a cabin projecting above the rail. Compare with express cruiser.

seiche Current on a lake.

seize To bind together using light line.

sedan cruiser

selective availability, S.A. The intentional degradation of a GPS signal by the U.S. Department of Defense for purposes of national security. The indicated positions are slightly inaccurate on commercial instruments.

self-bailing, self-draining Describes a boat, cockpit, or locker that automatically drains water.

self-righting See right.

self-steerer A device that steers the boat automatically. There are two types. The automatic pilot (autopilot) is an electrical device that steers a set compass course. A windvane steers the boat at a constant angle to the wind.

self-tacking Describes a sail that changes tacks automatically, without effort by the crew.

self-tailing winch, self-tailer See winch.

semidisplacement hull See displacement hull.

semidiurnal Twice daily. Once daily is diurnal.

sentinel See anchor.

separate rudder A rudder not attached to the keel.

serious Dedicated, flat-out. A **serious cruising boat** is usually well prepared for long-distance cruising.

serve To wrap light line around a wire splice to protect against corrosion and chafe.

set, to set 1) The **set** is the direction in which current pulls a boat. Compare with drift. 2) To **set a sail** is to hoist and trim it. A **sail's set** is its shape. 3) **Set the anchor,** see anchor.

settee A bench in a cabin. **A settee berth** can be converted into a berth.

720 rule, 360 rule See turns.

sextant, yoke The celestial navigation tool used to measure the angle to the sun or planets. The process is a **sextant shot.**

shackle A metal fitting that secures objects to each other. It is opened and closed using a clevis pin. A **screwshackle** uses a threaded clevis pin (screw pin). A **snapshackle** uses a quicker acting spring-loaded pin.

shakedown A familiarization run or cruise in a boat in order to "shake" all the problems out of her.

shake out See reef.

sharpen up, sharpen your wind See Head up.

shackle

sharpie A relatively narrow V- or flat-bottomed centerboard sailboat, sometimes with a cat-ketch rig.

she See boat names.

shear pin A light pin in a propeller system that breaks when the propeller hits an object. The failure of the pin saves the propeller from damage.

sheave Pronounced "shiv." See block.

sheer 1) The line of the curve of the rail from bow to stern. **Springy sheer** and **sweet sheer** are especially attractive, **reverse sheer** is convex and slightly humped, **flat (straight) sheer** has no curvature, and **split sheer** has two lines or angles either side of a break in the rail. The **sheerline** is the rail itself. 2) To swing or swerve, for example when at anchor in gusty wind. Sometimes, **sheer about.** 3) See wind sheer.

sheet The line used to adjust a sail's shape and angle to the wind. It is identified by its sail, for example **jibsheet, mainsheet.** To **sheet (sheet in)** is to trim a sheet. To **sheet a sail home** is trim until the sail is set properly. **Sheet stopper,** see lock-off.

shelter Protection from wind and waves. **Sheltered water** or a **sheltered harbor** is largely surrounded by land. Compare with open water.

shift A change in wind or current direction. A **shifty wind** is changing direction constantly. A **velocity wind shift** is a change in true wind speed that, because it affects apparent wind speed, allows a boat to head up or forces her to head off. See favor and wind.

ship 1) The largest type of vessel. Compare with boat. 2) To put something where it belongs. To **ship the oars** is to put them away.

shipmate A fellow crewmember.

ship's clock A clock that tells time with hands and also audibly with a system of bells or chimes on a four-hour cycle corresponding to the four-hour watch. "One bell" is 12:30, 4:30, or 8:30; "two bells" is 1, 5, or 9; and so on every half-hour to "eight bells" at 4, 8, or 12.

ship's gear Equipment carried or used by the vessel or her crew as a whole, for example a life raft for the entire crew. Compare with personal gear, which includes a PFD (personal flotation device) for an individual.

shipshape In good condition. See Bristol fashion.

ship's papers A vessel's official documents.

shoal(s) 1) An especially shallow area of water. 2) A **shoal-draft boat** has shallow draft.

shock cord Bungee cord, elastic rope.

shoe, lead shoe A quantity of metal (usually lead) that is fastened to the bottom of the keel in order to lower the boat's ballast and thereby improve stability.

shoot 1) To make progress toward a buoy, dock, or other object under momentum after the engine has been taken out of gear or the sails have been doused or luffed. The boat carries her way. 2) In celestial navigation, to take a sextant sight.

shore 1) The land, coast, or seaboard. **On shore** is on the shore or land. To go from a boat onto the land is to **go ashore**. **Shore power** is electricity used on board but supplied through an extension cord led to a plug ashore. 2) To **shore up** is to provide support.

short-ended Having short overhangs, with the bow and stern projecting only slightly. Compare with long-ended.

shorten sail, shorten down To reduce sail area by reefing or setting smaller sails.

short-handed With a smaller crew than usual.

shroud A sidestay. See stay.

shutter, storm shutter See storm.

shy Not quite dead ahead. To be **just shy of course** or of laying the mark is to be forced by wind or other reasons to steer to one side of the destination. **Sailing shy** is to sail on a close reach. A **shy kite** is a spinnaker used on a close reach.

side lights Port and starboard navigation lights.

sight reduction tables Published or computerized data used to make calculations in celestial navigation. See navigate.

silverware Prizes, trophies.

simplified racing rules See racing rules.

single-lever engine control The gear shift and throttle combined in one lever.

singlehanded With a crew of one.

single-sideband radio, SSB See radiotelephone.

sister ships Vessels built to the same design.

sit out British term for hike.

six-pack See certificate.

skeg In a boat's underbody, a fin running fore and aft just ahead of the rudder. It provides directional stability.

ski boat A boat designed for waterskiing, with an attachment point for the ski rope and a seat for a lookout.

skiff A small open boat.

skinny Describes a luffing sail. Compare with fat.

skipper The captain or person in charge of a boat's crew while she is under way. A **skippers' meeting** is a meeting for competitors before a race.

skylight A hatch admitting light below.

slack Loose, without pressure. To **slacken a sheet** is to cast it off. **Slack tide (slack water)**, see tide.

slalom ski A water ski designed for making hard, fast turns.

slam dunk In sailboat racing, a tactic whereby a boat on starboard tack closely crosses the bow of another boat on port tack, then tacks and covers the second boat in a way that leaves her no escape.

slant A wind shift. A **favorable slant** is a shift that works to the boat's advantage by lifting her. See lift.

slat 1) To roll or flap about in a calm. 2) See washboard.

sled A ULDB, ultra-light-displacement boat.

sleek A vague term suggesting "handsome" that landlubbers often fall upon when searching for a word to describe a boat.

sleigh ride A fast, exciting boat ride. Originally **Nantucket sleigh ride,** describing the towing of a whaleboat by a harpooned whale.

slicker Foul-weather gear.

sling A strap used to lift an object or person. See boatswain and Lifesling.

slip 1) A vessel's berth between two piers or floats, for example in a marina. 2) **Propeller slip,** see propeller.

slip the anchor rode Let the anchor rode run out so the boat can get away quickly in an emergency, for example in a rising storm or to avoid a collision. The rode usually will be buoyed so it doesn't sink.

sloop See rig.

slop A confused sea. **Sloppy conditions (sloppy seas)** are especially uncomfortable. See chop.

slot The gap between overlapping sails. The **slot effect** is the (much-disputed) beneficial effect that the forward sail may have on the after one.

slotted headstay, slotted mast A grooved headstay or mast.

slug, sail slug A bullet-shaped plastic or metal object sewn to the luff of a sail and fed into a grooved mast or headstay.

small-craft advisory A warning of potentially dangerous weather made by the National Weather Service, the Coast Guard, and other agencies. "Small craft" includes pleasure boats, yachts, tugs, barges with low freeboard, and other vessels with limited power.

small stuff Very light line.

SMG, speed made good See made good.

snap Describes a securing device that is easily opened and shut, for example **snaphank, snaphook, snapshackle**.

sniffer Bilge sniffer.

snore along Sail easily and comfortably on a reach.

snorkel A breathing tube extending above the water to provide air for a swimmer whose nose and mouth are submerged.

snorter A heavy wind or gale.

snotter A sail control that flattens a wishbone-rigged sail by adjusting the wishbone's position.

snub To take some of the strain off a line, for example by wrapping it around a cleat, winch, or other large fitting.

soft 1) Describes a sail that is luffing. Compare with hard. 2) A **soft spot** is a lull.

SOG, speed over the ground See made good.

solar panel A device that converts solar rays into electricity.

SOLAS See Safety of Life at Sea Conference.

sole The floor of the cabin or cockpit.

solid water The main body of a wave, as distinct from its spray.

sound, soundings To measure either the depth of water under the boat using a depthsounder or lead line, or the amount of fuel or fresh water in a tank using a rod (**sounding stick,** dipstick). **Soundings** are depth measurements. **On soundings** is an area of water relatively near shore and shallow enough to be sounded, generally inside the 100-fathom line. **Off soundings** is far offshore, beyond the 100-fathom line. See fathom.

sound signal, whistle signal, horn signal The sound made by a whistle or horn. Under the Navigation Rules, there are specific sounds that a boat makes with her horn or whistle to indicate her intended or ongoing maneuver. In a **two-whistle maneuver,** the boat turns so she leaves (passes) another boat on the latter's starboard side. In a **one-whistle maneuver,** she leaves the other boat on her port side. A **rudder-action signal** is a whistle or horn signal made at the time a turn is started. An **intent-agreement signal** signals one boat's intentions and the other boat's acknowledgment.

sou'wester 1) A fresh wind from the southwest. In some areas it is a **smoky sou'wester** because of the fog produced by the dampness it brings from the sea. 2) A waterproof hat with a large apron on the back to keep water off the neck.

spar A pole supporting a sail or rigging. Spars on a boat include the boom, outrigger, mast, gaff, spinnaker pole, and sprits. A **spar buoy** is a buoy with a tall pole.

Spectra Brand name for a polyethylene fiber.

speed A boat's or the wind's velocity. The **speed/length ratio (S/L ratio)** is the ratio between a boat's maximum speed and the square root of her waterline length. **Hull speed,** the theoretical maximum speed of a displacement hull (nonplaning hull), is determined by multiplying the square root of her waterline length by 1.34. See hull. **Speed made good, SMG;** see made good. A **speedometer** (knotmeter) is an instrument that measures and displays boat speed.

spi A spinnaker.

spindrift Spray blown from waves by a very strong wind.

Spinnaker, Parachute Spinnaker, Chute, Kite, Spi

A billowing nylon sail set forward of the headstay when running or reaching. There are two kinds:

- The **parachute spinnaker** has two leeches of equal length and is set on a **spinnaker pole** thrust forward from and to windward of the mast. It has two sheets. The one leading through the pole is the **spinnaker afterguy (spinnaker guy)**; the one on the other side is the **spinnaker sheet**.

parachute spinnaker

- The **asymmetrical spinnaker** has one edge longer than the other. It is set without a spinnaker pole. The tack is secured, either near the bow or bowsprit or to a sprit projecting from the bow. The clew has a sheet leading aft. When set it looks somewhat like a jib. On cruising boats it may be called a **cruising spinnaker**.

- Some spinnakers are designed and built for unique purposes. A

asymmetrical spinnaker

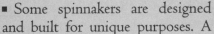

reaching spinnaker (shy kite) is cut more flat than a **running spinnaker**. An unusually small spinnaker set in strong wind is called a **chicken chute**.

A **spinnaker net** is a web of line hung in the foretriangle to prevent the spinnaker from wrapping around the headstay. A **spinnaker staysail** (cheater) may be set under the spinnaker to catch wind.

spitfire British term for storm jib.

splice To join two wires or lines, or to put an eye in a wire or line, by interweaving strands.

split pin See cotter pin.

split rig See rig.

split tacks To take a tack different from a competitor's.

spoke A handle on a steering wheel. The **king spoke** is the one that is vertical when the rudder is exactly centered under the boat.

sponson See cathedral hull and tunnel hull.

spoon bow A wide, shallow bow.

sportboat An especially lively, fast sailboat or powerboat no longer than about 25 feet.

sportfishing Fishing for swordfish, tuna, and other large gamefish offshore. A **sportfisherman** is a fast power boat equipped with a tuna tower, fishing rods, a fishing chair, and other fishing equipment.

spray Flying water. **Light spray** is like a fine rain. **Heavy spray** may severely obstruct visibility and the crew's activity on deck. See spindrift. **Spray chine,** see chine.

spreader, crosstree A strut on the side of the mast that holds out a shroud, thereby increasing its leverage on the mast in order to limit side bend. A **backswept (swept back) spreader** is angled aft to provide fore-and-aft support for the mast. A **spreader boot** is a rubber cap on the end of a spreader that protects sails from chafe. See stay.

springline, spring A docking line led forward or aft from the boat to the float or wharf to stop the boat from moving back and forth. Springs are laid out in pairs. The **forward spring** leads forward from the after part of the boat, the **after spring** leads aft from her forward part.

sprit A spar. When used on a mainsail or jib it is at an acute angle to the mast. See rig and wishbone boom. Some sprits are temporary bowsprits that extend forward of the bow to hold the tack of an asymmetrical spinnaker. Unlike a spinnaker pole, it is not raised on the mast. A **sprit boat** is a boat rigged this way.

squall A sudden local period of bad weather. A **wind squall** has more wind than rain, a **rain squall** more rain than wind. A **line squall** advances along a weather front. A **black squall** has unusually dark clouds, while a **white squall** wildly stirs up spray and rain.

square 1) Direct, see dead. 2) **Square rig**, see rig and tall ship.

squeeze To pinch.

squirrely Describes a boat that yaws or swings around so wildly that she cannot easily be steered on course.

SSB See radiotelephone.

stability Technically, a boat's tendency to return to her normal position, but usually refers to her resistance to heeling, capsize, rolling, and yawing. **Initial stability** (provided mostly by a wide beam) resists heeling and rolling at low angles of heel. **Ultimate (latent) stability** (provided by ballast) is resistance to capsize. A boat's **range of positive stability (stability range)** includes all the angles of heel at which she resists capsize. Once she heels beyond the upper limit of the range, she is likely to lose all stability and capsize. **Directional stability** (provided by a long keel and a skeg) is resistance to yawing, or steering off course.

staff See flagstaff.

stainless Stainless steel.

stall Separation of water or air flow from an appendage or sail, making the appendage or sail inefficient. Compare with attached flow.

stanchion See lifeline.

"stand by" Verbal alert to be prepared. **"Stand by to jibe"** warns of an imminent jibe.

standing part See line.

standing rigging See rigging.

stand on Hold course. Under the Navigation Rules (rules of the road), the **stand-on vessel** (also right-of-way vessel, formerly privileged vessel) is the one permitted to stay on her course in order to avoid a collision with another vessel. Compare with give way.

starboard Pronounced "star-bid." The right-hand side of the boat when the crew is facing the bow. When a sailboat is on the **starboard tack,** the wind is coming over the **starboard side.** Compare with port.

start 1) To **start sheets** is to ease the sheets in a sailboat when heading off on a reach. 2) The beginning of a race. The **starting sequence** is the series of audible and/or visual signals that indicate the start of a race.

stateroom An unusually large sleeping cabin.

station Location. The **navigator's station** is where the navigator works, the **steering station** where the steering wheel and instruments are located. The **maximum beam station** is the point along the hull of the boat's maximum width.

STAY, SHROUD

A length of wire (wire rigging), steel rod (rod rigging), or other low-stretch material that supports a mast and adjusts its bend.

- Some stays run forward to support the mast against falling aft. Some of these also hold up sails: the **headstay (jibstay),** which runs from the bow to the top or near the top of the mast, and the **forestay (inner forestay)** (not found on all sailboats), which runs from the deck partway between the mast and bow and inside the headstay. The **babystay** runs just forward of the mast to control its lower sections; it does not carry a sail. **Jumper stays** run aloft up the forward side of the mast over jumper struts.

- **Backstays** run aft from the mast to the stern or the after quarter to keep the mast from falling forward. The **perma-**

nent backstay (backstay) is permanently installed and runs from the stern to the top of the mast; a **split backstay** is arranged on a bridle to make room for the tiller. A **backstay adjustor** is a block and tackle or hydraulic system that adjusts the backstay's tension. **Running backstays** (runners) go partway up the mast on the starboard and port sides and may be adjusted and disconnected at the deck.

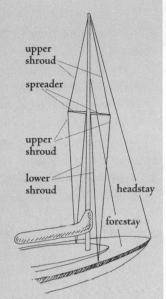

- The other type of stay is the **shroud (sidestay)**, which provides sideways support for the mast. Shrouds run from the side decks up the side of a mast. Many run over spreaders. **Lower shrouds** (lowers) connect below the lower spreaders, **intermediate shrouds** (intermediates) higher up, and **upper shrouds** (uppers, **cap shrouds**) connect to the mast at or near its top. **Discontinuous shrouds** terminate at spreaders rather than bend over them. **Diamond shrouds** (diamonds) also run along the side, both ends terminating on the mast. **Shroud rollers** are tubes placed over shrouds to let sheets and sails slide by easily.

staysail Pronounced "stay-sul." A small sail, often set inside or below another sail. A **forestaysail** is a small jib set on the forestay. A **spinnaker staysail** (cheater) is a lightweight small jib set under a spinnaker. A **mizzen staysail** is a lightweight sail set on a yawl's or ketch's mizzenmast when reaching or running.

steadying sails, riding sails Small sails set on powerboats and sailboats to limit rolling in waves.

steaming light, bow light See navigation lights.

steer To aim a boat. When using a reference point, for example a star or a compass, one **steers by** it. Steering is done with the helm, which is either a tiller or a **steering wheel.** The helm is at a **steering station,** which may be outdoors in the cockpit or fly bridge or inside in a pilothouse. **Steering cables** are wires connecting the steering wheel to the rudder.

steerageway See way.

steerer, helmsman, helm The person steering a boat; sometimes a helms*man*. The **steerer's (helmsman's) seat** is a seat behind or near the steering wheel.

stem The bow's forwardmost edge or tip. The **stem (anchor) roller** is a roller for the anchor rode. **Stem to stern** is the length of a boat; to **search stem to stern** is to inspect the entire boat.

step To install a mast in a boat, with its bottom (the heel or butt) inserted in the **mast step.** A **keel-stepped mast** has its mast step on the boat's bottom, a **deck-stepped mast** has its mast step on deck.

steps A series of ridges on the bottom of a powerboat that help her plane.

stern The back (after) end of a boat, including the after underbody, the counter, the afterdeck, and the transom. If cut off flat across in a transom it is a **transom stern,** if pointed it is a **canoe stern** and the boat is a double-ender. To moor or anchor **stern-to** is to put the stern nearest the wharf or drop the anchor over the stern. **Stern drive,** see inboard/outboard drive. **Stern light,** see navigation lights.

sternway A boat's backward motion. Compare with headway.

stiff Strong. A **stiff boat** has good stability. A **stiff breeze** is a strong wind.

stock The vertical post in a rudder or anchor.

stock boat, stock design, production boat A boat or design that is often reproduced. Compare with custom boat.

---

stop 1) To tie thread (**stopping twine**) or loop rubber bands around a sail before hoisting so it does not fill prematurely. 2) A **sail stop**; see sail.

stopper A lock-off.

storage A boat's location when she is not being used in the off season. **Dry storage** is on land and indoors, **wet storage** is in a berth in the water.

stores, ship's stores Supplies.

storm Wind of 48 knots or greater. **Storm sails** (see sail) are the **storm jib** and the **storm trysail,** which takes the place of the mainsail but is set without the boom. A **storm shutter** is a board fastened over a window or port to block waves. **Storm anchor,** see anchor. **Storm tactics** are decisions made about courses or rigs to ride out storms, gales, and heavy weather. They include heaving-to, lying ahull, setting storm sails, **running with a storm,** scudding, and deploying a drogue or sea anchor. **Storm alert (storm watch, storm warning),** see weather alert.

stow, store To put away an object where it belongs. **Stowage** is a locker, bin, or other location in which to stow objects.

"straight up and down" Report when weighing anchor that the rode is vertical and the bow is over the anchor.

strake A strip of wood, fiberglass, or metal on the outside of the hull. On the topsides, **rubbing strakes** rub against wharves or other boats to prevent the sides from being scratched. On the bottom, **running (lifting) strakes** limit rolling and push spray to the side.

stream To pay out a line over the stern.

strike To lower quickly. To **strike colors** is to lower the ensign at sunset.

stringer A structural support for the hull running fore and aft in the bilge.

stripped out Having very minimal accommodations.

strobe light, strobe An especially bright, intense blinking light installed on some aids to navigation and also used to attract attention in emergencies. A **masthead strobe** is at the top of the mast and is illuminated to draw another crew's attention when a collision threatens. A **personal strobe** is a small emergency strobe light carried by an individual in case she or he falls overboard.

strong wind Wind of 22 to 27 knots.

structural Important to the boat's strength. A **structural member** is a frame, stringer, beam, keel, or other part of the boat that contributes to her strength.

stuffing box, packing gland A fitting at the through-hull for the rudder stock or propeller shaft that provides lubrication and minimizes leaking.

suction area The area immediately aft of a large moving vessel where the wash pulls objects toward the vessel.

suitcase, valise See life raft.

suit of sails The sail inventory.

sump A cavity in the bilge for collecting water. It has its own pump, the **sump pump.**

sunbridge See express cruiser.

superstructure The hull, cockpit, deck, bridge, and other major components of a boat outside the rig.

superyacht See megayacht.

surf To ride down the face of a wave.

surfacing drive, surface-piercing drive See propeller.

surge 1) The motion of a wave or water. **Storm surge** is the unusual rise of water caused by a strong onshore wind. 2) To move back and forth, for example at anchor or when docked as the anchor rode or docking lines stretch.

survey To examine a boat closely for structural weakness. The job (a **survey**) is done by a professional **surveyor.**

survival conditions Weather so dangerous that the boat may sink or be severely damaged.

survival suit An especially heavy, buoyant dry suit that keeps a wearer both warm and afloat in the water for extended periods. Compare with dry suit and wet suit.

swage To squeeze a terminal fitting onto a wire under very high pressure in order to connect them. The result is a **swaging**. For example, to connect a stay to a turnbuckle, a terminal fitting is **swaged onto** the stay, and one end of the fitting is secured in the turnbuckle's jaws. Compare with nicopress.

swallow-tailed Describes a flag with a V-shaped back edge.

swamp To fill with water due to capsize or waves.

sweating Water condensation on the inside of the hull and deck.

swell Long, regular waves. Compare with groundswell.

swim platform, swim ladder A platform on the transom near the water, or a ladder rigged temporarily on the boat's side.

swing For a boat to move about at mooring or anchor. **Swinging room (swinging radius)** is the open area needed around the anchor so the boat does not collide with other boats as the wind and current shift. Sail around the mooring (anchor), see sail.

swing table, gimbaled table A table with gimbals, which keep it level as the boat heels or rolls.

swivel A fitting on a block or shackle that allows it to rotate fully.

tabernacle A hinged on-deck mast step. It allows the mast to be lowered easily.

tabling Cloth reinforcement on the edge of a sail.

tack 1) A sailboat's heading relative to the wind. Unless she is headed into the wind, a sailboat is always on a tack. On **starboard tack** the wind comes over the starboard side, on **port tack** it comes over the port side. "The" may be used before "tack," but "a" is never used. For example a boat sails **on port tack** or **on the port tack,** but not on a port tack. 2) To **tack** (**change tacks,** come about, go about) is to head up through the eye of the wind, and then head off with the wind on the other side. To **tack through** an angle is to inscribe that angle while tacking. 3) The lower forward corner of a mainsail or jib; the corner of a spinnaker near the spinnaker pole. To **tack down** a sail is to secure its tack to its fitting.

tackle, block and tackle, handy billy Traditionally pronounced "*tay*-kul." A system of blocks through which line is rove. It increases hauling power. The sections of line between the blocks are parts, and the pulling end of the line is the fall. The number of parts determines the power of the tackle, less friction. For example a **four-part tackle** has a purchase of

slightly less than 4:1; a
10-pound pull on the
fall should lift a weight
of almost 40 pounds.
A **handy billy** is a tackle ready and available

four-part tackle

for any use. A **relieving tackle** is a tackle led to the tiller or
steering wheel to facilitate steering in rough weather.

tactician The crewmember in a racing boat who decides on the
courses to take and maneuvers to make.

taffrail The rail at the stern. **Taffrail log**, see log.

tail To pull on the end of a line that is under load. The **tailer** is
the person who does the pulling. See winch.

take on, take aboard To bring something or someone aboard
a boat. To **take on (take aboard) fuel** is to put fuel into the
tanks. To **take on water** may mean either to fill the water tank
or to leak. To **take on crew** is to bring on new crewmembers.
A boat **takes a wave aboard** when a wave breaks on her deck.

tall buoy A mooring buoy with a tall rod that may be easily
picked up from the deck of a boat.

tall ship A square-rigger, or square-rigged sailing ship, used for
training or commerce. See also rig.

tang A metal strap on a spar for securing a block or stay.

tank A permanently installed container for water, fuel, or
sewage. A **holding tank** is for sewage; see marine sanitation
device.

tank test, model test A test of the potential speed of a design
by pulling a small model through water and measuring
resistance.

T-bone When one boat rams another amidships at a right angle.
The worst kind of collision.

T.D., time difference See Loran-C.

telltale, woolly A short length of yarn or ribbon on a stay or
sail that indicates wind direction and assists in sail trim.
Telltale compass, see compass.

tender 1) Describes a boat that heels easily. 2) A small boat that carries crew and supplies to and from a larger boat.

terminal fitting, rigging terminal A metal fitting attached to the end of a stay or other wire in order to connect it to a turnbuckle, the deck, a spar, or other object.

tether See safety harness.

the See boat names.

thimble A metal or plastic eye spliced into the end of a wire or line. When a shackle is inserted, the thimble protects the line or wire against chafe.

three sheets to the wind Drunk.

360 rule, 720 rule See turns.

throat In a gaff rig, the forward end of the gaff, usually in the shape of jaws that slide up and down the mast. The **throat halyard** raises and lowers the throat.

throttle Accelerator on an engine.

through-fastened Bolted, not screwed.

through-hull, thru-hull A water intake, water drain, transducer, propeller shaft, rudder shaft, or other object in a hole in the bottom or side of a boat. A seacock or stuffing box usually is fitted to prevent leaks and close the hole if the fitting fails.

throw rope, throw bag, throw sock See heaving line.

thruster Bow thruster. See bow.

thwart A seat running across a dinghy or other small boat.

'thwartships See athwartships.

TIDE, TIDAL CURRENT

tide The vertical rise and fall of the oceans, seas, and their extensions due mainly to the gravitational pull of the moon and sun.

- **High tide** is the highest level, **low tide** the lowest. Mean high water (MHW) and mean low water (MLW) are the average **heights of tide**. **Tidal range** is the average difference in feet or meters between MHW and MLW.

- The **flood tide** is the rising, incoming tide when the **tide floods (is on the flood, is flooding)**. Contrarily, the **ebb tide** is the falling, outgoing tide when the **tide ebbs (is on the ebb, is ebbing)**. **Slack water (slack tide)** is when there is no ongoing **tidal change**.

- **Spring tides** are especially high and come during the new and full moon; they have nothing to do with the season. **Neap tides** come at the quarter moon.

- **Tide changes** usually follow a regular diurnal (one tide change daily) or semidiurnal (two daily) schedule. A **tide table** is a printed or electronic publication showing the times of high and low tide and other tidal information, usually excepting currents. A **tidal clock** displays the tide schedule in a clocklike format.

tidal current Horizontal water movement caused by the tides rather than by the wind (wind-driven current).

- **Maximum tidal current** usually is halfway between the times of low and high tide, **minimum tidal current** is at the very beginning or end of the tidal cycle. A **tidal current table** provides the time, speed, and direction of tidal current.

- A **tide rip (tide race, tidal race)** is an area of especially rough water caused by fast-moving tidal currents running either over shallow water or in conflict with each other, and often helped by a strong wind.

tie-down A line or other device for holding something in place.

tight Taut, straight. A **tight (straight) leech** on a sail does not curve. Compare with loose.

tiller The rod that turns the rudder to steer the boat when there is no steering wheel. A **tiller extension** (hiking stick) is a hinged extension on the tiller that permits steering from off to one side. An **emergency tiller** is installed if the steering wheel breaks.

time allowance Corrections to the elapsed times (times taken by competitors to finish a sailing race) and used to handicap the performance of boats of different size. See handicap and rating rule.

tongue weight See trailer.

toerail A low footbrace.

toggle A U-shaped metal fitting that, when its jaws are closed by a clevis pin, links a stay's turnbuckle with its chainplate. The toggle permits movement so that the turnbuckle is not bent when the stay shakes or is out of line.

tooling The molds and plugs used to build a boat.

topping lift A line or wire that holds up a boom, spinnaker pole, or other spar.

topsail Pronounced "topsul." See sail.

topside On deck.

Top-Sider A brand of deck shoes.

topsides The sides of the hull above the waterline.

torque See propeller.

tote bag An open-topped canvas bag. See ice bag.

tournament A fishing competition.

tow To pull. A boat **under tow** is being pulled by another.

track 1) A boat's course made good as drawn on a chart. See made good. 2) A boat that **tracks well** has good directional stability and holds her course without too much work by the steerer. 3) A length of metal on which jib leads, cars for travelers and spinnaker poles, and sail slides move.

trade winds, trades Predictable seasonal ocean winds relied on by commercial sailing vessels.

traditional boat, character boat Wooden boats, vessels with square or gaff rigs, and pleasure boats derived from workboats or fishing boats. Examples are the catboat, lobster boat, and trawler. **Traditional appearance (traditional lines)** is the look of sailboats and powerboats designed before about 1960 and of more recent boats inspired by them. Those boats usually have at least a few of the following characteristics: wooden construction, low freeboard, narrow beam, heavy displacement, long overhangs, long keels, short masts, divided rigs, and fractional rigs. See classic.

traffic separation scheme A pattern of one-way shipping lanes laid out to separate vessels in shipping channels and crowded waterways.

trailer, trailerable To **trailer (trail)** a boat is to pull it on a trailer behind a vehicle on the highway. A **trailerable boat** or **trailerboat** is a boat that can be readily trailered. The **trailerboat rig** is the trailer, boat, and accompanying gear. The trailer consists of an axle, wheels, boat supports, warning lights, and a tongue hooked to the towing automobile's **trailer hitch**. The downward pressure at the hitch is the **trailer tongue weight**.

transceiver Radio receiver and transmitter.

transducer An electronic sensing device in the bottom of the boat, usually in a through-hull, that provides the data for a boat's depthsounder or speedometer.

transformer A device that changes 120-volt electrical current to 12-volt current. Compare with inverter.

transom A flat surface running across the stern. A boat without a transom is double-ended and has a pointed stern. A **transom stern** is raked aft, a **reverse transom** is raked forward. An **open transom** has large holes to save weight and allow water to drain aft. A **notched transom** has a recess in the hull near the stern to improve water flow near the propeller and allow the propeller to be raised slightly. See counter, rake, stern.

Transpac A sailboat race from Los Angeles to Hawaii held in odd-numbered years.

trapeze In smaller racing sailboats, a wire hanging from the mast that supports a crewmember who is standing outboard in order to improve stability.

traveler An athwartships track with an adjustable block (the car) that controls the athwartships set of a sail.

Travel-Lift A vehicle that hoists, hauls, moves, and launches boats at boatyards.

trawler A heavy-displacement powerboat inspired by commercial fishing boats. Trawlers with a fine finish and cruising accommodations are **trawler yachts.**

trawler

tricolor See navigation lights.

trim 1) To pull on a sheet. 2) The attitude of a boat. **Trimmed (down) by the bow (stern)** means that the bow (stern) is lower than desired. **Trim tabs** are flaps at the powerboat's stern that are adjusted so the boat rides level. 3) The condition of the sails and boat. A boat **in good trim** is in good shape. A **well-trimmed sail** has the right shape. 4) Wooden detailing.

trimaran, tri A boat with three distinct side-by-side hulls, the center one larger than the others. The side hulls (outriggers, floats, amas) are attached to the center hull (vaka) by a bridge, struts, or crossbeams (akas). The design originated in Polynesia. A **folding trimaran (tri)** can be folded up so it is sufficiently narrow to be trailered. Compare with cathedral hull and tunnel hull.

trip, trip line Disconnect remotely. To **trip the anchor** is to break it loose from the bottom by pulling straight up on a **trip line** attached to it. **Trip lines** are also used to open fittings from a distance.

troll To fish while the boat moves very slowly. A **trolling engine** is an especially small gasoline or electric outboard motor (kicker) carried for this purpose.

trotline A line used to moor several small boats or to pull a boat to shore.

true direction Geographical direction ignoring the earth's magnetic field and oriented toward the geographic North Pole and South Pole. Shown on the compass rose on a chart. Compare with magnetic direction.

true wind The actual direction and strength of wind, as felt on a boat that is not moving. Compare with apparent wind.

trunk The cabin above deck.

trysail, storm trysail See sail and storm.

T-top A canvas or other fabric cover over the helm to protect the steerer. Compare with hardtop.

tumblehome The curve of the topsides toward the deck.

tuna tower A high platform in a fishing boat from which spotters look for fish. A low platform is a marlin tower.

tuna tower

tune To adjust an engine, rig, sail, or rigging until it is at optimum performance. **In tune** is to be at peak performance.

tunnel hull A powerboat with one or two low tunnels in the bottom, extending the length of the hull from bow to stern. The side hulls (sponsons) are not as distinct as the hulls in a catamaran or trimaran but are more distinct than the ones in a cathedral hull.

turn A wrap of a line around a cleat or winch.

turnbuckle, rigging screw A device for adjusting tension, usually in a stay. It consists of threaded rods joined by a threaded barrel, plus jaws to attach it to the deck and the stay.

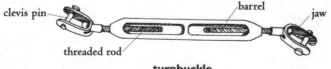

clevis pin   barrel   jaw

threaded rod

turnbuckle

turning radius, turning circle The distance required for a boat to turn around.

turns, 360 rule, 720 rule In sailboat races, boats that acknowledge that they have violated the racing rules may take a penalty by sailing in circles while their competitors sail on.

turtle, turn turtle For a boat to turn upside down.

twin engines, twins Two engines.

twing, tweaker A control line for a spinnaker sheet.

twin jibs, twins Two jibs set on cruising boats on either side of the headstay when the boat is running before the wind. With the mainsail lowered, a boat rigged with twins will steer easily.

twist The curve of a sail's leech to leeward.

two block To raise a halyard all the way.

two-stroke A two-cycle outboard motor.

Type I-V See PFD (personal flotation device).

ULDB, ultra light-displacement boat, sled An extremely lightweight sailboat that is especially fast when sailing before the wind. Popular in California, where many races are downwind.

una rig, unirig See cat rig.

under A boat's situation. A boat that is **under way** is moving, **under tow** is being pulled, **under sail** is sailing, **under full sail** is sailing with all possible sails set, **under power** is being propelled by her engine, and **under bare poles** has no sails hoisted.

underbody, canoe body The area of the hull that lies below the water.

undercanvassed, underpowered Having sails or an engine that are too small for best performance. Compare with overcanvassed and overpowered.

underrigged With a mast and other rigging that are too small or light. Compare with overrigged.

unfair Rough. An **unfair hull** is gouged or bumped.

unidirectional Describes a fiberglass material or sailcloth yarn that is especially strong in one direction so it resists stretch along that line.

Uniform State Waterway Marking System, USWMS The buoyage system for many small lakes and rivers. It uses elements of both the cardinal and lateral systems.

United States Coast Guard, USCG/U.S. Coast Guard Auxiliary, USCGA See Coast Guard.

United States Offshore Racing Association The organization that governs offshore powerboat racing.

United States Sailing Association, U.S. Sailing, USSA The organization governing sailboat racing in the United States. Formerly the United States Yacht Racing Union (USYRU) and the North American Yacht Racing Union (NAYRU).

uppers See stay.

upwind To windward.

U.V., ultraviolet rays The sun's rays.

V-berth, vee-berth Twin berths in a forward cabin that are joined near the bow as the boat narrows.

V-bottomed, vee-bottomed, veed sections Describes a boat whose bottom is V-shaped, with high deadrise (the bottom's angle to the water). In powerboats, a **deep-V** has about 26 degrees of deadrise all the way from bow to stern, while a **modified-V** has a sharp V at the bow, then gradually flattens toward the stern. Compare with flat-bottomed and round-bottomed.

deep-V

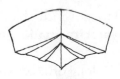

modified-V

V-drive An arrangement in which the propeller shaft is installed at an acute angle to the engine rather than on a straight line (direct drive).

vaka See trimaran.

valise See life raft.

vang A line or tackle that helps control a spar. A **vang** on a gaff pulls the gaff to windward. A **boom vang** keeps a boom from lifting.

variable Shifty, unsteady in direction and force.

variation The difference in degrees between true north and magnetic north. Variation varies from area to area and year to year. It is shown on a chart's compass rose. See compass.

veer 1) To ease a line is to **veer it out.** 2) A clockwise wind shift. Also haul. When the wind shifts from north to east it **veers** (hauls) or is a **veering** (hauling) **wind.** Compare with back.

velocity Speed. **Velocity wind shift,** see shift. A **velocity prediction program (VPP)** is a computer program that predicts a boat's speed on all points of sail in different wind strengths.

ventilator, vent An air scoop on deck. The scoop is called a cowl. One type is the **Dorade ventilator,** which has internal baffles that stop water from passing below. It was first used in the ocean racer *Dorade* in 1930.

vessel Any ship, boat, yacht, canoe, or other floating object with room for one or more people.

VHF-FM Very high frequency radiotelephone receiver and transmitter. See radiotelephone.

visibility The clarity with which, and the distance at which, an object can be seen. **Poor visibility** includes times of fog and dense rain. The **range of visibility (visibility range)** is the distance at which objects can be seen.

VMG, velocity made good Speed made good (SMG). See made good.

voyage A long offshore trip that eventually returns the vessel to the starting point. Compare with passage.

VPP, velocity prediction program See velocity.

VTIS, Vessel Traffic Information System An electronic information and warning system used in congested waters.

wake The path of waves stirred up by a moving boat. A **no-wake zone** is a body of water where low speed limits are enforced in order to keep wakes small. Compare with wash.

walk See propeller.

walkaround A small powerboat with a low deck around the cabin.

walkway A narrow fore-and-aft pathway near the rail.

warning, hurricane (storm) warning See weather alert.

warp A heavy towline or mooring line. To **warp a boat in** is to move her into a dock or slip by hauling on the docking lines.

wash Disturbed water caused by a moving vessel. Compare with wake.

washboard, hatchboard, slat A removable plastic or wooden slat installed in a hatch or companionway to prevent water and wind from going below.

watch 1) Hurricane (storm) watch, see weather alert. 2) An assigned group of crewmembers that alternates boathandling and lookout duties with another group (or other groups) according to a schedule. The process is **standing (keeping) watch.** There usually are two watches, the **starboard watch** and the **port watch.** The one on duty is the **on watch,** the one off duty is the **off watch**. The **watch is changed** when they swap. The **watch captain** is the crewmember in charge of a watch. The **midwatch** is on duty between midnight and 4 A.M., when the **dawn (morning) watch** comes on deck. An **anchor watch** keeps a lookout when the boat is anchored. To **dog the watch** is to follow an irregular schedule for a short period of time so the watches do not stand at the same hours each day and night.

water 1) The water around the boat. **Broken water** has ripples or waves, **raw water** is the water pumped into the boat to cool the engine. 2) The water in the boat, the **ship's water** or **fresh water**. A **water tank** is a metal or fiberglass container for water, built into the boat. **Water ballast,** see ballast.

waterfront The commercial part of the shore, often with wharves, piers, and docks.

waterline The boat at the water's surface. Also the horizontal line between the points at the bow and stern where the water surface touches the hull. Compare with boottop. **Waterline length (LWL),** see length.

waterlogged So saturated with water that there is almost no buoyancy.

watermaker, desalinator A device that converts salt and other impure water into drinkable water.

waterman A commercial fisherman.

water taxi A launch.

watertight bulkhead, collision bulkhead See bulkhead.

waterway A river, creek, canal, or small lake.

wave Undulations on the water's surface caused by wind and current. Very small waves are ripples, large ones are seas. A **bow wave** is stirred up by the bow, a **stern wave** by the stern. The **wave train** is the pattern and direction of the waves. **Breaking waves** (breakers) have tops that are unstable and fall over. A **rogue wave** is unusually high.

way A boat's motion. A boat in motion is **under way (has way on)**. **Headway** is forward, **sternway** backward. **Steerageway** is sufficient speed so the boat can be steered; below that speed the rudder is ineffective. To **take way off** a boat is to stop her. A boat **carries her way** when she has momentum after the sails are doused or luffed or the engine is taken out of gear.

waypoint A destination or intermediate point on a passage. Its position may be stored in the memory of a GPS or other electronic navigation device, which calculates the course and distance (range and bearing) to the waypoint.

ways At a boatyard or shipyard, a marine railway on which a vessel is hauled out of the water.

weather 1) Generally the climate, but usually taken to refer to local conditions of wind and sea. In **heavy (rough) weather** winds are strong, waves steep and large. In **calm (flat) weather** there is very little wind. **Nasty (bad) weather** is uncomfortable, **fair (good, fine) weather** is comfortable. A **weather cloth,** a wide strip of fabric, is tied to the lifelines to keep spray out of the cockpit in heavy weather. **Weather eye,** see eye. 2) **To weather** is upwind, to windward.

weather alert, weather advisory, weather watch, weather warning In anticipation of storms, hurricanes, and other heavy weather, the National Weather Service uses and broadcasts three levels of alerts: advisory, watch, and warning. A **weather (storm) advisory** identifies the existence of hazardous weather. A **weather (storm) watch** is an alert to a possible threat. A **weather (storm) warning** is an alert to an expected threat.

weatherfax A facsimile machine that prints weather maps.

weather helm See helm.

weatherly Able to sail close to the wind.

weather saying An epigram that summarizes a weather observation, for example "The sharper the blast, the sooner it's past"; and "Red sky in morning, sailor take warning, red sky at night, sailor delight."

weekend To go out in a boat for a two- or three-day cruise. A **weekender** is a boat with only modest accommodations.

Compare with cruise and overnight.

weigh anchor To raise the anchor. When it is **aweigh** it is off the bottom.

wet See dry.

wet locker Stowage area for wet foul-weather gear and other damp clothing.

wet suit Tight rubber clothing that allows water between it and the skin. The body maintains its heat by warming the layer of water. Compare with dry suit and survival suit.

wetted surface The surface area of a boat's underbody and appendages.

wharf An area along the shore on a waterfront where vessels tie up. Compare with pier.

wheel Steering wheel, but sometimes propeller.

wheelhouse Pilothouse. See pilot.

whip 1) To **whip the end of a line** is to lace it tight with light line (**whipping twine**) so it won't unravel. 2) A single block with a line rove through it, providing 2-to-1 purchase.

whisker pole A spar used to hold out a jib when sailing wing-and-wing.

whistle signal See sound signal.

Whitbread Round the World Race A sailboat race starting and finishing in England.

whitecap The foam at the top of waves in a fresh wind.

wildcat See windlass.

Williamson turn A method for turning a large vessel around. First turn 60 degrees off course, then put the helm hard over in the other direction until the boat is on the course reciprocal to the original course.

williwaw A gust of wind blasting down a hillside onto the water.

winch A drum turned either manually with a crank called the **winch handle** or by electricity, to pull sheets, halyards, and other lines (but not ground tackle, which is the job of the windlass). To increase their power, many winches have two or more gears (**two-speed winch, three-speed winch,** etc.). A **self-tailing winch** (self-tailer) automatically secures the line as it is being pulled in. See grinder. **Primary winch,** see primaries.

WIND, BREEZE, AIR

Moving air. Although wind is created by complex changes in the weather and local geography, it is conveniently described as blowing from a source. The **wind direction** is the direction from which the wind blows. A **southwest wind** blows from the southwest, a nor'easter from the northeast. A **prevailing wind** is the wind that usually blows.

■ **Upwind** (**to windward,** to weather) is in the direction toward the wind's apparent source (opposite of **downwind**).

■ A **heavy wind** (**strong wind, heavy air**) blows more than 22 knots. **Windy** describes a strong wind. **Light wind** (**light air**) blows less than about 10 knots.

■ **Dirty wind** (**dirty air**) is wind affected by another boat or object, for example by covering or backwinding. **Clear** (**clean**) **wind** (**air**) is unaffected. To be **on another boat's wind** or to cover her is to give her dirty wind.

■ To sail **on the wind** is to sail close-hauled, **off the wind** is to be on a reach or run.

■ A **wind shift** (**slant**) is a change in the wind's direction. See shift.

Wind sheer is the difference between the wind velocity and direction at the deck and aloft. See apparent wind and true wind. A **wind generator** is an onboard propeller that generates electricity. **Wind indicator,** see apparent wind.

windage Surface exposed to the wind.

windchill An indicator of cooling of the body due to the combination of air temperature and wind. In the United States windchill is expressed in degrees Fahrenheit, in Canada in watts per square meter.

Windex A popular brand of masthead fly (apparent wind indictor).

windlass A drum, turned manually or by electricity, for pulling the anchor rode. It usually has a specially shaped drum (the wildcat) for hauling chain.

window Besides the usual meaning, a clear portion in a sail, through which the crew can see to leeward.

windscoop, windsail A cloth scoop that catches wind and passes it through a hatch to provide ventilation below.

windscreen A clear plastic surface at the forward end of the cockpit or fly bridge.

windseeker A light sail used in very light winds and drifting conditions.

windsurfing, Windsurfer See sailboard.

windvane See self-steerer.

windward, upwind, weather Toward the wind. To **beat to windward (upwind, to windward)** is to sail close-hauled, as close to the wind as possible. The **windward (upwind, weather) side (rail)** is the side or rail closest to the wind. Compare with leeward.

wing, wing deck An extension of the deck outboard from the hull. In a trimaran the wing, called the **wing deck** or bridge deck, connects the hull with the two outboard hulls. The **underwing** is the under side of the wing deck. An especially narrow wing is a crossbeam.

wing-and-wing Sailing on a run with sails set to both sides. The jib is **wung out** or poled out on its side by a whisker pole or spinnaker pole.

wing keel, winged keel See keel.

wing mast, wing sail A mast, sail, or combination of the two shaped like an airplane wing. If the mast is large and the attached sail is small, the mast is a **wing mast**. If the mast and sail form a single wing-shaped structure it is a **wing sail**. Wing masts or sails are aerodynamically very efficient but complicated and expensive. They usually are found in sophisticated racing catamarans or trimarans.

winterize To prepare a boat or engine for winter.

wire rope Steel wire filaments twisted to form flexible cordage-like lengths.

wishbone boom, wishbone rig Replacing the traditional boom, curved sprits side by side on either side of a sail and joined together at a point well up the mast and at the sail's clew. They hold the sail out and down. This is the rig used on sailboards. See snotter.

wishbone rig

woollies Telltales, which sometimes are made of yarn.

workboat A small commercial boat that serves the needs of other vessels, for example as a launch, towboat, etc.

workboat

working sails See sail.

wung out See wing-and-wing.

yacht 1) Historically, and still the case in most countries, a pleasure boat of any size and type. **Yacht racing** is the sport of racing sailboats. 2) In the United States, the word yacht often is applied to a pleasure boat longer than about 40 feet with luxurious accommodations. 3) A better and more typical definition applies a higher standard: to be a yacht, a pleasure boat must be unusually graceful, well proportioned, and seaworthy in appearance, and have a fine paint or varnish finish. Luxury is less important than ability. 4) Increasingly, the word is also used to describe any large powerboat that takes passengers for pleasure, including cruise ships. 5) Related terms. A **yachtsman** or **yachtswoman** is someone who owns or uses a yacht under any of these meanings. A **yacht broker** is a professional seller of boats. A **yacht club (Y.C.)** is a private organization of boaters; most yacht clubs have waterfront facilities, marinas, and anchorages. A **yacht designer** is a naval architect who specializes in designing yachts. **Yacht ensign,** see ensign.

yard, yardarm The horizontal spar in a square rig or in a yacht club's flagpole. Evening is falling when **the sun is over the yardarm.**

yarn-tempered sailcloth Dacron sailcloth that has been treated to make it especially resistant to stretch. The sail is stiff, almost like light metal.

yaw To steer a weaving course. See stability.

yawl See rig.

Y.C. Yacht club. See yacht.

zebra mussel A thumbnail-size freshwater crustacean. It reproduces rapidly. Masses of them clog water intakes.

zinc, sacrificial zinc, zinc block, zinc anode A small piece of zinc metal that is secured to or placed near the underwater part of an outboard engine, metal hull, or other metal object in salt water. By attracting galvanic activity, it protects the engine, hull, and other objects from corrosion.

Zulu, Z Greenwich Mean Time (GMT). The time at the Greenwich meridian, or zero degrees longitude.